Table Set

....

COOKING WITH

Tamika Scott

A TASTE OF THE SOUTH IN YOUR MOUTH

FOOD PHOTOGRAPHY BY ZAVIER DE'ANGELO
ADDITIONAL PHOTOGRAPHY BY:
PRINCESS ARMANI, AND DARNELL "BAE" WINSTON
COVER DESIGN BY: RACHAEL NICOLE TURNER

HUNTER PUBLISHING

Cooking withTamika Scott
©2022 Tamika Scott
Publishedby: Hunter Publishing
Food photographs and chapter-opening photographs, unless otherwise credited,
copyright ©2022 by Hunter Publishing

All rights reserved
ISBN: 978-1-7327002-7-7
Ebook: 978-1-7327002-5-3
Mass distribution: 978-1-7327002-4-6
Library of Congress number: 2021924183

Edited by: Keyoka Kinzy and David Good
Cover Design: Rachael Nicole Turner
Interior Layout: Ni'cola Mitchell
Creative Director: Sharina Nicola
Food Photography: Zavier De'Angelo, Princess Armani, and Darnell "Bae" Winston

Dedication

I am forever grateful for all who have sown into my life Spiritually, Mentally, and Creatively! To everyone who took out time from your busy schedules to taste, enhance, give your honest feedback, or just blessed me with your presence, I Thank You! To my grandmother Mildred Ponder, my mother Gloria McFarlin, I am the woman I am today because of the women you are and have always been. Thank you for being perfect examples of loving Wives, Mother, and Grandmothers. I Love You Both, dearly! Daddy, thank you for teaching Latocha and I how to be treated as little princesses and making sure we knew how to do everything a man could do and more! I Love You and will forever be daddy's little girl! To my sisters, brother, aunts, uncles, cousins, thank you for the fond memories and the love you have given me throughout the years. I Love You! And yes, My Family Is Everything!

To my incredible husband, Darnell Winston, thank you for your unconditional love and patience with me. Thank you for believing in me when I didn't believe in myself. I Love you immensely! You are my heartbeat. To my beautiful daughters, Oshun, Taniyah (Young Niyah), and Princess Armani, everything I do is for you! I'm beyond grateful that God chose me to be your mother. Mommy Loves you with all my heart! To my glam babies, Aveyah, Aria, and Prince Cason, Glam-Ma Loves You! To My Incredible Team, whom I call family, Jayda Atkinson, Allan Cole, and Steve Thompson, thank you! It's been a journey, and you have been right by my side every step of the way! Words cannot express how appreciative I am for each one of you. This is only the beginning!

Ra-Phael Blanco, thank you my friend for being the best PR who ran with the torch and diligently made this book deal happen! You're the man! Yvette Hayward, thank you for being the connector to this entire puzzle. You're the bomb.com! Nancey Flowers, A.K.A Fancy Nancey, thank you for pushing me beyond my limits and encouraging me to tell my stories the way I wanted to! Thank you for the long drive to make sure everything was immaculate for me in every way.

Hunter Publishing, we did it! Thank You, Thank You, Thank You for giving me EVERYTHING I asked for and more! You have gone above and beyond what a publishing company provides! My experience with you has been an author's dream! You took my vision and made it into an exceptional masterpiece. Thank You for allowing me to share my love, family, friends, and experiences with the world. I am forever appreciative of everything you have done. You're more than Hunter Publishing to me; you are now and will forever be my family! Thank You!

Dedication

Table of Contents

iamreginalove When is the book coming out Sis 🤤🤤🤤🤤🔥🔥🔥
27w   Reply

 thekenyamoore ✔ OMG👏👏👏👏
1d   3 likes   Reply

 luvaltheaheart ✔ best ive Ever tasted!! 🔥🔥
19w   4 likes   Reply

 iamreginalove My Sis is an Amazing Cook 🔥🔥🔥 @therealtamikascott
42w   1 like   Reply

 dr_heavenly ✔ Mmmmm mmmmm!
19w   4 likes   Reply

 darlenemccoy ✔ Sis ... ummmm..... why u be doin this to us ?🔥🔥🔥🤤🤤🤤🤤
2w   70 likes   Reply

 yannasoulsings ✔ My Goooodness!!!!!!!! Jesus my mouth started watering!!😂😂😂
2w   38 likes   Reply

 antwontanner2214 ✔ 😋😋😋😋😋
34w   9 likes   Reply

 trinabraxton1 ✔ This food was Delicious! @vonscales and I enjoyed it immensely! Do it again tomorrow! 😀🔥🖤

 itowandabraxton ✔ I'm coming over!!!
22w   19 likes   Reply

shaniceonline ✔ 🖤🖤🖤🖤🖤🖤🖤 That looks good sis
10w   15 likes   Reply

 yannasoulsings ✔ My lord!
10w   3 likes   Reply

 therealleleeswv ✔ Gil ur house is a whole restaurant 😂
3w   92 likes   Reply

 kandi ✔ That looks good!!!
45w   62 likes   Reply

 dr_heavenly ✔ Ooooohhhh😭😭
28w   7 likes   Reply

 iamlatocha ✔ When you said Crockpot, I thought about when Mama G would prepare the greens in the am, and let them simmer in that crockpot until after church. BABY!!! You talkin' about some good eating!!! Sis. You betta!! We get it from our Mama 🖤🖤🖤

 luvaltheaheart ✔ 🔥🔥🔥 Can't wait for your book
27w   19 likes   Reply

 niccigilbert ✔ Yuuuuummm
17w   3 likes   Reply

 themamamiax ✔ 🖤🔥🔥🔥🔥🔥
37w   7 likes   Reply

 **rodneyperrylive** ✔ Squash casserole looks crazy my wife is a half vegan i need to make her that

 iammsbotalley ✔ I'm coming over DANG IT
37w   5 likes   Reply

 617mikebiv ✔ Go get em sis ...
27w   14 likes   Reply

Table Set

COOKING WITH

Tamika Scott

A TASTE OF THE SOUTH IN YOUR MOUTH

Introduction

I was born and raised in Georgia, in a tough little city known as College Park. My father, Randolph Scott, was a Deacon at our church and a Police officer in Clayton County, Ga. He taught my sister, Latocha, and me how to protect ourselves, how to be disciplined, and how to stand up for what was right, even if we're the only ones standing. My mother, known to all as Mama Gloria, was the undisputed heavyweight champion of all housewives! So, when I say Perfect, Loving, Devoted, Generous, Unselfish, (and the list goes on) Mother you would ever meet. Together my parents were "The Power Couple," living the American dream.

While my dad was hard at work policing, my mom worked hard at home, helping my sister and me with our homework and school projects, taking us to choir rehearsals, and keeping the house sparkly clean (you could practically eat off our floors), and preparing dinner nightly. My mom cooked dinner every night, and we sat down at the dinner table as a family and shared stories of our day, having good old fashion family time over a delicious meal. You could feel the love in our dining room. This made me daydream as a little girl. I would close my eyes and see myself as a wife, sitting with my husband and two daughters, eating a delicious home-cooked meal prepared by yours truly. To be half of the mother/wife my mother was, I knew I had much learning to do. I watched my mother like a hawk, mimicking everything she did. I would watch her cook and ask millions of questions. She was so patient with me, answering every last one of them.

The best part of being in the kitchen with my mother was the fact that she would let me help her cook. From getting the eggs and buttermilk out of the refrigerator for her cornbread, to helping her remove the husk and silk from an ear of corn; pulling greens from the stalk and soaking them in vinegar and salt to clean, to scaling and cleaning fish we caught at the lake, my mom taught me and allowed me to learn by cooking with her. As a result, I can proudly say I cooked my first three-course meal all by myself at the age of 13. This Book is a result of all that I've learned by watching, remembering, and practicing

Author's Note........

    My life was moving at a fast pace, touring with my music group X-scape, acting in a live stage production with Lolita Snipes "Head Over Heels," working on my first solo project, "Family Affair," running my label, Brolic Entertainment, overseeing my daughter's, Young Niyah, acting and rap career, being a wife, a mother, and a Glam-ma. My plate was full until March 16, 2020. We were out celebrating my husband's 48th birthday eating at a restaurant with family, when all of a sudden, my sister, Latocha, came in wearing a face mask. I laughed so hard when I saw her. She didn't think anything was funny. "You never watch the news, do you?" She asked. I not only skipped out on the news, I don't even watch tv, period.

I made a couple more jokes about my sister's mask until we left the restaurant. My baby girl, Princess Armani, talked about a project due by the end of the week on the way home. We stopped by the store to purchase several items for her school project. I looked around to see if anybody was wearing a mask like my sister had on earlier. Nope, not one person had on a mask. We gathered the things Princess Armani needed and headed home. I ran her bathwater and turned on the tv in her room to look at the news. The news anchor vaguely touched on a new virus known as Covid-19 and mentioned it as a common cold or flu. I turned the tv off and continued getting Princess Armani ready for her bath just in time for a meeting with my singing group X-scape and our managers, discussing upcoming shows. After agreeing to do the dates presented to us, I received an email from Princess Armani's school.

The email stated there would be no school for two weeks because a teacher had contracted Covid-19. This made us start looking deeper into the virus. President Trump did a press Conference and reassured us the virus wasn't as severe as people claimed it to be. But the next day, it seemed the world stood still. Everything was closing early, all of the food was being bought out, Princess Armani's piano lesson had been canceled, her gymnastics, her ballet, and jazz classes as well.

What was going on? I had no clue. I got a call from my mother telling me to go to the store and get tissue, milk, water, meat, cleaning products, and everything I needed to last me and my family for a good month because of the virus. I went to the store as soon as it opened. My husband and I filled two shopping carts with everything everyone in the house liked to eat and snack on. We had enough essentials to last us for a few good months, just in case what my mom said was true. As soon as we were walking out of the store, people were everywhere, practically rushing inside. I was so glad that I didn't hesitate because everything was gone when I returned later that day to get some hot sauce. OMG... For the first time in years, I was home with my husband and kids, in the house watching the news and trying to figure out what was about to happen next. After binge-watching every news channel, I began to get depressed. I left everyone sitting in the family room watching tv, and I went into the kitchen. I stood in front of the stove and let out a big sigh.

Our home was full of emotions. I knew exactly how to relieve everyone for a moment. I went to the refrigerator and took out the butter and eggs. I went to the pantry and took out the baking soda, sugar, all-purpose flour, and semisweet chocolate chips. I could hear my family discussing their feelings about the virus and not doing things they had planned. The tension of the uncertainty of how one could catch the virus and the number of individuals that contacted it, and the number of deaths of those who did was causing my family to stress. I said a silent prayer and began preparing everyone's favorite, homemade chocolate chips. I put them in the oven, and the sweet aroma made everyone come into the kitchen. Immediately the conversation shifted from the news to what was in the oven. Everyone began smiling and making requests for dinner the next day and the next and the next. Since I was going to be home, they all wanted their favorite foods cooked. The next day everyone woke up to a big breakfast. I made homemade potato fries, scrambled eggs, creamy grits, fried chicken strips, and buttery biscuits. I set the table up the way I would if we had company. They were all surprised. My daughter shared it on her social media, and her messages were flooding with likes.

Later I prepared a full course meal and shared it on my social media. Immediately, everyone was messaging me asking me what spices I used for frying my fish and what I used to make my hush puppies and what I put in my broccoli casserole. I answered every message. The next day, I cooked again, updated my fans on how my family and I were doing, and checked in on them. Later that day, I posted another picture of the meal I had prepared, and the messages came in like a flood. It took me an entire day to respond to all of them. By the fourth day, my fans told me how impressed they were that I could cook and that everything looked delicious. They also said I should do a cookbook. Ok, my husband tells me that all of the time, and I always brush him off. But now, I was getting this from my fans.

People who loved my singing and acting. I never thought they would embrace me as a home chef, but I was wrong. The more I cooked and posted, the more messages I received. I finally listened to my husband and my fans and wrote a cookbook and shared my favorite recipes with everyone. Now I have the time. Cooking is my therapy. Whenever I get stressed out about anything, I channel that energy into creativity. Cooking is how I relieve stress and also the way I show my family and friends Love. This began the journey of my cookbook.

Check In!

I want to see all of your photos from gathering ingredients to right before you dive in! Tag me on your posts!

@TheRealTamikaScott
#CookingWithTamikaScott

Tour Life 2 Home Life

Most of you know me for being a member of the R&B group X-scape. I have been blessed to tour all over the world with my childhood friends. We've been everywhere; you name it! Germany, Paris, Japan, Amsterdam, Canada, Mexico, Hawaii, and the list continues. When my group and I are on stage, we have perfect harmony, but when it comes to agreeing on what we're going to eat, metaphorically, we're off-key and out of sync.

My sister, Latocha, and Tiny (Tameka Harris) are vegans. Kandi and I are meat-eaters. Can you imagine being in one van and going to only one place? We could never agree on a restaurant that would satisfy us all.

(Me and Kandi on one side, Latocha and Tiny on the other). Unfortunately, the hotels we stayed in didn't have kitchens in the rooms. If we returned to the hotel too late, the restaurants would be closed, resulting in going to bed hungry. It took a few arguments and disappointments for us to decide on hiring a catering company.

Even then, the food wasn't always satisfying. The chicken was dry at times; the vegetables were over cooked and under seasoned, there were food items we didn't request, and for the items asked were omitted. I couldn't wait to get home in my kitchen to cook EVERYTHING I was craving on tour.

On the first day back home from the tour, my family had so many requests. They were tired of eating out daily and were longing for a home-cooked meal prepared with love.

I was jetlagged, tired, aggravated, and burnt out. None of that mattered because I missed my family, and I was happy to be home. I allowed two food items per person to be requested. My baby girl, Princess Armani, wanted her favorite, Mama Mika's Meatball and Spaghetti. Young Niyah wanted Shrimp Fettuccini Alfredo with my homemade Pop Biscuits. My oldest daughter, Oshun, wanted Grilled Salmon and my Garlic, Long Legged Asparagus, and my husband wanted some loving, with a side of Broccoli Casserole and my mouth-watering Butternut Squash. Believe it or not, they all agreed on dessert, Peach Cobbler. Just seeing the smiles on my family's face made me forget how tired I was and gave me the much-needed energy to cook everything they asked for, along with dessert.

They all sat in the kitchen, watching me cook and filling me in on what was going on in their lives since I had been away. Laughter filled the kitchen, and the love was overwhelming. Oh, how I missed my babies and how I missed cooking and hearing the "mmm" sound after every bite. As I looked into everyone's eyes, it reminded me of why I work so hard! I want my kids to have a better life than I did. No sacrifice was or is too big to keep them happy. So, if cooking three meals a day allowed us to sit as a family and eat together and communicate without interruptions, I would do what I have to do for the beautiful memories and unconditional bond we have!

Broccoli Rice and Cheese Casserole

Ingredients

2 cups of cooked rice
(2) 12 oz. fresh or frozen
broccoli florets (steamed)
Chopped
2 tablespoons of butter
½ cup of minced onions
1 cup of milk
(1) 10 ½ oz. can of condensed
Cream of chicken soup
(1) 10 ½ oz. can of condensed
cream of mushroom soup
2 tablespoons Tamika Scott's
"All- Purpose" Southern Fuse
2 cups of Kraft's, Philadelphia,
creamy
melt mild cheddar
1 cup of Kraft's, Philadelphia, creamy
melt sharp cheddar
1 Tablespoon of Tamika
Scott's "Cajun" Southern Fuse

Directions

1. Preheat oven to 350°F. Butter a medium greased pan.

2. In a large pot over medium-high heat, melt butter. Add onions and cook until translucent. Stir in both cans of soup, milk and Cajun Fuse. Mix well and cook for 5 minutes. Remove pot from heat/ burner.

3. Combine cooked rice, steamed broccoli florets, All purpose Fuse, 1 cup of sharp cheddar cheese and 1 cup of mild cheddar cheese to the soup mixture. Stir until well incorporated.

4. Spoon mixture into a greased pan. Cover with foil and bake for 20 minutes.

5. Remove from the oven, uncover and sprinkle remaining mild cheddar cheese evenly on top.

6. Return dish to the oven uncovered, bake 10 minutes or until cheese completely melts.

7. Let cool, serve, and enjoy.

Ingredients

1 lb. of asparagus
1 lemon (juice)
1teaspoons of minced garlic
3 tablespoons of olive oil.
*1 tablespoons of Tamika
Scott's "Vegetable" Southern
Fuse*
*2 tablespoons of parmesan
cheese*

Directions

1. Over medium heat, in a large skillet, add olive oil and garlic—Cook 1 minute stirring.
2. Add asparagus, season with 1 tablespoon of Vegetable Fuse, add lemon juice. Let simmer for 5 minutes, turn asparagus, and season with "Vegetable" Fuse
3. Add lemon juice. Cover and let simmer for 4-5 minutes. Add parmesan cheese on top. Serve and enjoy.

Georgia "Peach" "Cobbler"

Ingredients

1 ½ cup of Bisquick
1 (29 oz.) can of sliced peaches in heavy syrup
¼ cup of peach syrup from the can
1 cup of milk
1 ½ cup of sugar
½ cup of butter (to melt in a casserole dish)
¼ cup of butter (for mixture)
1 teaspoon of cinnamon
½ teaspoon of nutmeg
½ teaspoon of Tamika Scott's "Sweetener" Southern Fuse
½ cup of Brown Sugar
1 tablespoon of vanilla extract

Directions

1. Preheat oven to 350°F.
2. Melt ½ cup of butter in a casserole dish. Take out of the oven when the butter has melted.
3. In a big bowl, mix ¼ cup of butter, peaches, ¼ cup of peach syrup, ½ cup of sugar, vanilla extract, brown sugar, nutmeg, cinnamon, and Sweetener Southern Fuse. Spread over melted butter in a casserole dish.
4. In the same mixing bowl, add 1 cup of sugar, milk, and Bisquick together until you have a smooth mix.
5. Pour mix over peaches. Bake for 40-45 minutes or until golden brown.
6. Let stand for 12 minutes before serving. Enjoy with Ice cream or just by its delicious self.

Cajun Shrimp and Broccoli Fettuccini Alfredo

Ingredients

(1) 12 oz. box of Fettuccine noodles

1 ½ lb. large shrimps, peeled, deveined, and cleaned

½ lb. lobster bites (cooked)

1 ½ cup of broccoli florets (Steamed)

(3) 32 oz. carton chicken broth

2 teaspoons minced garlic

2 tablespoons of Tamika Scott's "Seafood" Southern Fuse

2 tablespoons of Tamika Scott's "Cajun" Southern Fuse

2 Tablespoons Tamika Scott's "All-Purpose" Southern Fuse

½ cup of milk

1 pint of heavy whipping cream

3 tablespoons of butter, divided

1½ cup freshly grated parmesan

2 tablespoons olive oil

Directions

1. In a large cast-iron pot, bring chicken broth, All-purpose fuse, one tablespoon of olive oil to a boil. Add noodles and stir, cook for 5 minutes stirring, Cook until al dente. Reserve 1 cup of noodle water to thicken the sauce, if needed.
2. Drain noodles, set aside.
3. In a large skillet over medium heat, melt one tablespoon of butter, add one tablespoon olive oil, add garlic, stir. Add shrimp. Season with Seafood Fuse. Cook 3 minutes per side.
4. Take shrimp out put it aside. Turn heat to medium-high. Add two tablespoons of butter, whipping cream, milk, Cajun Fuse, All-purpose Fuse in the same skillet. Stir, cover, and bring to a boil. When sauce thickens, add parmesan. Stir, and allow the cheese to melt. (If the sauce isn't thick as you like, add a tablespoon of all-purpose flour)
5. Add lobster bites, shrimp, and broccoli. Stir and cover for 10 minutes.
6. Add noodles to the sauce, stir to coat evenly. Serve and enjoy

Ingredients

For Meatballs
1 ½ lbs. of ground beef OR 1 lb. ground beef & ½ lb. of ground pork
1 cup of Italian style breadcrumbs
½ cup of (fresh grated) parmesan cheese
2 large eggs
½ cup of water
½ cup of ricotta cheese
1 ½ tablespoon of Tamika Scotts "All-Purpose" Southern Fuse
1 teaspoon of minced garlic

For Meat Sauce
(Feel free to use your favorite store-bought spaghetti sauce or try mine)
1 lb. ground beef
2 tablespoons of Tamika Scott's "Beef" Southern Fuse
(1) 29 oz. can, crushed tomatoes
(1) 6 oz. of tomato paste
(1) 29 oz. can tomato sauce
One yellow onion (diced)
½ cup of your favorite barbecue sauce
½ cup of sugar
1 teaspoon of black pepper
2 tablespoons of Tamika Scott's "Vegetable" Southern Fuse
1 package of spaghetti noodles
1 Tablespoon olive oil
(3) 32 oz. beef broth
(2) 32 oz. chicken broth

Directions

1. Preheat oven to 350°F. Prepare meatballs for the stove.
2. In a large bowl, mix 1 ½lbs. ground beef with breadcrumbs, parmesan, ricotta cheese, eggs, minced garlic, and All-Purpose Fuse. Use your clean hands to combine, adding water gradually until the eggs have mixed thoroughly.
3. Roll mixture into a perfect ball. We are placing in oven baking dish. You can roll them in large balls or medium size.
4. Bake 10 minutes; turn and bake for 8 more minutes or until golden brown.
5. While Meatballs are baking, prepare noodles. Add beef, chicken broth, and "Vegetable" Fuse in a large pot over medium to high heat. Bring olive oil and noodles (I break mine in half over the broth, then place in the boiling water). Cook according to the package. When done, drain and set aside.
6. While noodles are boiling, In a big skillet, brown 1lb. Ground beef, onion, 2 tablespoons of "Beef" Fuse. Drain fat from meat.
7. Add tomato paste, tomato sauce, diced tomatoes, barbecue sauce, sugar, and black pepper to browned meat. Stir, cover, and bring to a boil.
8. Take the meatballs out of the oven and place them in sauce and simmer for 5 minutes. Turn meatballs and simmer for 5 more minutes.
9. Serve sauce over noodles and enjoy

Ingredients

1 lb of Salmon Fillet
1 Tablespoon of butter
2 Tablespoons of Tamika Scott's "Cajun" Southern Fuse
1/4 cup of soy sauce
1/2 cup of brown sugar
3 teaspoons of minced garlic

Directions

1. 1. Preheat oven to 350 Fahrenheit. Season both sides of Salmon with Cajun Fuse.

2. Line a baking dish with aluminum foil. Lay butter in the middle of the foil. Place Salmon on top of butter. Fold up the sides of the aluminum foil around the salmon.

3. In a small bowl, mix soy sauce, brown sugar and garlic. Pour mixture over salmon. completely close aluminum foil and bake for 15-20 minutes.

4. Serve and enjoy!

Ingredients

4 cups of Bisquick
1cup of sour cream
1 cup of 7-Up soda
½ cup of melted butter
½ cup of sugar
2 tablespoons of honey
1 cup of powder sugar

Directions

1. Preheat the oven to 400°F. In a large bowl, combine Bisquick, sour cream, 7-up, sugar, and honey.
2. Knead and fold dough until mixed well. (If too sticky, sprinkle Bisquick onto surface and pat dough out." Cut circles out of the dough using a biscuit cutter or rim of a small glass.
3. Add butter to a large baking dish. Put in oven to melt. Take out and sprinkle with powder sugar.
4. Place biscuits on top of melted butter. Bake 15-20 minutes, or until biscuits are golden brown.

Ingredients

2 lbs. of butternut squash, peeled, seeded, and cut in ¾ inch cubes

1 Tablespoon of Tamika Scott's "Sweetener" Southern Fuse

1Tablespoon of brown sugar

2 Tablespoons of Maple syrup

Pinch of Salt and pepper (to taste)

Cooking spray

Directions

1. Pre-heat oven to 400°F. Grease sheet pan with cooking spray.
2. Mix brown sugar, Sweetener Fuse, maple syrup, olive oil, and salt and pepper in a large bowl.
3. Place squash cubes in a mixture a few at a time to coat evenly.
4. Arrange squash cubes in a single layer on the greased pan.
5. Drizzle half the sweet mixture over the squash. Place in oven and cook for 15 minutes.
6. Turn over the squash and drizzle with the remaining sweet mixture. Cook 15 more minutes or until your desired tenderness.

I was told as a little girl that eating carrots made your vision better, hair longer, and boost your immune system. Bugs Bunny, the animated cartoon character, made it look so cool to eat carrots. I wanted to keep my 20/20 vision, grow longer hair, remain healthy, and look fabulous while eating it. I couldn't get past the texture and taste of this odd-looking vegetable. It didn't matter if it was raw or cooked; I didn't like it. I tried eating it with ranch dressing, which is my favorite. That didn't make it any better. My mom wanted to disguise it in her homemade chicken noodle soup, and it was always left in my bowl, followed by, "Mommy, I'm full."

One day after church, my family and I went to Morrison Cafeteria. This was the restaurant where my parents met. They loved telling us the same story over and over again about how they worked together there and fell in love. Morrison reminded me of my school cafeteria, where you stand in line, grab your tray, and walk behind the person in front of you. I was looking at multiple choices of food and the labels. You tell the person standing behind the glass which items you wanted; they would grab it, then reach under the glass and hand it to you. My parents allowed me and my sister to get only one sweet item. I loved Jell-O, and that was always my go-to dessert.

On this particular day, I walked through the line and noticed the sweet potato casserole was labeled as carrot soufflé. I didn't know what soufflé meant, but I knew what carrots were, and this side dish wasn't carrots. I got it before my mom could see me. She was in front of the line with my sister, and I was standing in the back of the line with my dad. He was talking to everyone around us, so I knew he wasn't paying attention. If my mom asked me why I had sweet potato and Jell-O, I would tell her that it was labeled carrots, and I didn't know it was sweet potatoes.

My father helped us take the food off of the trays and handed them to the waitress. I sat next to my dad, and when he took my tray, I placed my sweet potatoes next to him, so if my mom looked over, she wouldn't think they were mine. My dad blessed the food, and I started digging in. My mom looked over at me and smiled. I was glad she overlooked the sweet potatoes. My dad looked down at my sweet potato. "Are these yours?" I shook my head yes, slowly not looking up to see his expression. He pushed them closer to me. "Glad to see you eating your vegetables." He smiled. Even he was fooled by the label. It wasn't until I finished eating all of my food is when I found out that I was eating carrots. Thinking I was fooling my parents, the joke was on me. I'm glad I didn't know I was eating carrots because I never would've tried it, and I would've missed out on this delicious vegetable.

Ingredients

2 lbs. of carrots
½ cup of (salted) butter, (soften, room temperature)
4 eggs
1 teaspoon vanilla extract
1 teaspoon of salt
¼ cup of all-purpose flour
1 ½ teaspoon of baking powder
1 cup of sugar
1 tablespoon of sugar Cooking spray
Powdered Sugar (for garnish)

Directions

1. If using can carrots, drain juice from the can. Add carrots to a medium saucepan. Cover with cold water.
2. Add salt and 1 tablespoon of sugar—Cook over medium to high heat. Bring to a boil—cover and cook for 30 minutes or until tender.
3. Preheat oven to 350°F.
4. Grease a baking dish/ pan with cooking spray.
5. Drain carrots. Add cooked carrots to a food processor. Process until mixture is smooth.
6. Add butter, sugar, vanilla extract, and eggs to the processor. Process until incorporated.
7. Add baking powder and flour to the processor. Pulse until combined.
8. Spoon mixture into the greased baking dish. Cook 45-50 minutes or until soufflé is set. Take out of the oven. Allow cooling for 5 minutes.
9. Add powdered sugar on top. Serve and enjoy!

One thing my husband and (adult) kids have in common is not wanting to try different foods. Their mind set is, if they didn't like it as a child, they will not like it now. I sat down and had a serious conversation with them about opening up their minds and taste buds to embracing new foods, especially vegetables. They agreed until I said the star vegetable was Squash. "SQUASH!" My husband smirked, raising his eyebrows. Then he followed that outburst with a challenging phrase, "I Don't Even Eat My Mother's Squash!" Wait A Minute!!!!! Did he just challenge me? Oh yes, he did.

From that very moment I vowed to make him eat his words and my squash! A week later I whipped up my Southern Squash Cheesy Casserole and put it on his dinner plate with his favorite vegetable, broccoli, along with his favorite meat, baked chicken. He was watching the game and wasn't paying attention when I sat his plate in his lap. After saying a short prayer, he dug into his plate. I didn't want to make a scene so I walked backed in the kitchen waiting to hear if he would complain or not. My daughter, Niyah, had just finished making her plate as I entered. She admired the melted cheesed on top of the casserole. "This looks delicious! What is it?"

I smiled as she took a bite. "MMM this is really good Ma. What is it?" I smiled and said not a word. I wasn't ready to reveal what she'd just eaten until I heard from my husband. Minutes later he came into the kitchen with a clean plate. "Baby that was delicious! Make me another plate please." I smiled even harder. "I want both of you to know," I said, "that you just ate Squash!" I danced around my husband and repeated his words, "I don't even eat my mother's squash." All he could do was smile back at me. He hit me on my behind and said, "Make me another plate!"

Tamika's Southern Squash "Cheesy" Casserole

Ingredients

2 lbs. (4 medium) yellow squash

1 can (10.5 oz) Cream of Chicken Soup

½ can of Milk

½ medium Onion (Diced)

2 cups of Shredded Mild Cheddar Cheese

1 tablespoon of Tamika Scott's "Vegetable" Fuse

Cooking spray

Directions

1. Preheat Oven to 350°F. Spray baking dish with cooking spray.
2. In a large pot, combine Cream of Chicken Soup and milk. Simmer on low heat, whisking often, until creamy.
3. Add chopped onions, yellow squash, Vegetable Fuse. Gently stir, cover, and let Simmer for 2 minutes. Take off burner.
4. Sprinkle evenly a half cup of shredded cheese on the bottom of greased casserole dish.
5. Add soup and squash mixture in casserole dish. Sprinkle ½ cup of cheese. Stir Bake (covered) for 20 Minutes.
6. Sprinkle remaining cheese on top of casserole. Put back in the oven (uncovered) for 5 minutes or until cheese is completely melted.
7. Let sit for 5 minutes and enjoy.

Chicken Chicken Chicken

Chicken is Princess Armani's favorite food in the whole world. She will eat chicken "Every day" if I let her. I'm constantly reinventing ways of making her favorite dish so the rest of us won't get tired of it. Please believe me when I say I could write a cookbook on "100 Ways or More to Make Chicken", thanks to Princess. On career day, Princess Armani's teacher asked her what she wanted to be when she grew up, and Princess said she was going to own her restaurant that sells chicken twenty-four hours a day. Her teacher thought that was the funniest thing. Her entire class laughed at her. When Princess came home, she was a little upset.

She asked me to go to the store and get her a few notebooks so she could use them to write down her recipes for the restaurant she wanted me to open up for her. After explaining how she felt when her teacher and classmates laughed at her, she was ready to go to the store. I had to hold my laugh in and try to keep a serious face. Mind you, Princess Armani was only six years old at the time. She rode with me to the store and continued to vent. "I'll show them! They better not come and try to work for me neither. I won't hire anyone who thinks my ideas are dumb!"

I told her never to let anyone destroy her dreams. No matter how crazy it may sound to someone else. I tried to encourage her and get her in a better mood. After hearing a few songs on the radio that she liked, she was feeling a lot better. Princess bought five notebooks, went home, sat at the table, and wrote for at least an hour. Every day after that, she wrote in her book. She created the name of her company, her menu, her rules and regulations (which were too cute to me) and made a diagram of how she wanted her restaurant to look. At 8, Princess has incorporated the name for her business; we've purchased almost every appliance she will need and are now looking at buildings. She is ahead of her time. I dedicate this part of my book to her. Because every recipe is Princess Armani approved!

Ingredients

6 boneless chicken breasts
(2) 10 ½ oz. cans of
condensed Cream of Chicken
Soup
2 cups of chicken broth
2 cups of rice (uncooked)
Tamika Scott's "Poultry"
Southern Fuse
1½ tablespoon Tamika
Scott's "All-Purpose" Fuse

Directions

1. Preheat oven to 375°F.
2. In a large baking dish, stir in the soup, broth, rice, and All-Purpose Fuse.
3. Season both sides of chicken breast with "Poultry" Fuse.
4. Place chicken breast on top of the rice mixture and cover with foil. Bake 45-50 minutes or until chicken is complete. Allow the chicken and rice to sit for 10 minutes.
5. Stir rice, serve, and enjoy.

Pop'n Peppered Chicken

Ingredients

4-6 boneless, skinless breast
2 bell Peppers
2 red Peppers
2 large yellow onions, sliced
2 cups of your favorite
barbecue sauce
8 oz. Coke
½ Cup of ketchup
½ Cup of brown sugar
1 tablespoon of maple syrup
Tamika Scott's "Poultry"
Southern Fuse (preferred
amount)
1 Tablespoon of "Tamika
Scott's "Barbecue" Southern
Fuse
(This dish taste even more
delicious after marinating
overnight)

Directions

1. Preheat the oven to 400°F.
2. Clean chicken breast and pat dry.
3. Season chicken breast on both sides with the preferred amount of Poultry Fuse Seasoning.
4. Slice up Onions, red peppers, and bell peppers.
5. Place half in a roasting pan.
6. Place chicken breast on top of vegetables.
7. Add the rest of the vegetables on top of the chicken.
8. Combine ketchup, maple syrup, brown sugar, barbecue sauce, Coke, and "Barbecue" Southern Fuse in a medium bowl. Stir.
9. Pour mixture over chicken. (Cover up with foil and let marinade overnight for a wow factor) or cover and bake for 30 minutes.
10. Turn chicken over to the other side, cover with aluminum foil, and place in the oven for 20 more minutes or until chicken is done.
11. Serve and enjoy.

Honey Barbecue Chicken

Ingredients

2 lbs. of party wings
2 cups of flour
2tablespoons Tamika Scott's
"Barbecue" Southern Fuse
1 cup of your favorite
barbecue sauce
½ cup of honey
Oil (The oil of your choice for
deep frying)
½ cup of "less sodium" soy
sauce
1 Tablespoon of hot sauce
2 Tablespoon of brown
sugar

Directions

1. In a deep fryer or large frying pan, heat oil to 375°F.
2. Combine barbecue sauce, honey, soy sauce, hot sauce, and brown sugar over medium heat in a small saucepan. Cover, and bring to a boil. Stir, turn the heat down to low and allow the sauce to simmer.
3. In a large bowl, combine flour and Barbecue Fuse.
4. Add wings a little at a time, tossing to coat.
5. Fry a few party wings for four to five minutes on each side or until the chicken has browned and is thoroughly cooked.
6. Drain on paper towels.
7. Transfer wings to a large bowl and add sauce. Toss to coat. Serve immediately

Lemony Peppered Wings

Ingredients

4 lbs. of party style chicken wings

1 cup of all purposed flour One teaspoon of sea salt

2½ tablespoons of Tamika Scott's "All-Purpose" Fuse

1 Lemon

Oil for frying

¾ cups of butter

2 tablespoons of Tamika Scott's "Lemon Pepper" Southern Fuse

Directions

1. Add oil to the fryer or large frying pan. Set fryer to 350°F.
2. Preheat oven to 350°F. Add flour and All-Purpose to a medium bowl. Coat chicken in flour. Make sure to shake off any extra flour. Lay the chicken on a nonstick cooling rack. Repeat until you cover all the chicken with flour.
3. Once the temperature of your grease has reached 350°F, begin frying a few pieces at a time. Don't crowd the fry basket or the pan. Fry for 7 minutes or until it is golden brown. Take out of grease and lay them on a paper towel to drain. Repeat until all chicken is finished.
4. Put chicken in the oven for 10 minutes.
5. Melt butter and add half of a lemon's juice to butter and stir. Next, add your dry Lemon Pepper Fuse to the butter, and stir.
6. Remove chicken from the oven. Get your medium-size bowl. Put a few chicken pieces into the bowl, pour a little lemon mixture on the chicken, and toss, toss, and toss until the mixture is well incorporated. Do this again until all chicken has been based in the Lemon Pepper Fused butter mixture. Add a few sliced carrots and celery sticks with your favorite dipping dressing and enjoy.

Princess Armani's Parmesan Chicken

As you already know, Princess Armani drives me crazy with her love for chicken. This is a quick and easy recipe that she loves to help make. I don't know what she likes better, mixing the breadcrumbs and parmesan cheese with her gloved hands or eating it.

Ingredients

4 boneless, skinless chicken breasts
½ cup mayo
¾ cups panko breadcrumbs
⅓ cup of parmesan cheese, shredded
Tamika Scott's "Poultry" Southern Fuse
1 teaspoon Tamika Scott's "All-Purpose" Seasoning (mayo mixture)
1 teaspoon Tamika Scott's "All-Purpose" Southern Fuse (parmesan mixture)
Cooking spray

Directions

1. Preheat oven to 400°F. Grease a 9 x 13-inch baking pan. And dry chicken breast. Season each side with Poultry Fuse and set aside.
2. In a small bowl, stir together mayonnaise and one teaspoon All-Purpose Fuse.
3. In the 2nd bowl, add panko breadcrumbs, parmesan cheese, and one teaspoon All-Purpose Fuse. Lightly stir to incorporate.
4. Coat each side of chicken breast in a mayonnaise mixture.
5. Next, press both sides of the chicken breast in a parmesan mixture.
6. Place chicken in greased baking pan.
7. Repeat with remaining chicken and place each piece in the baking pan.
8. Lightly spray the top of the chicken with cooking spray. Cover with foil. Place in oven for 20 minutes.
9. Remove foil and bake for 25 more minutes or until completely done.
10. Remove from oven and allow it to sit for 5 minutes.

My family and I rarely eat out. I try to cook every day but on this particular Tuesday, we all went to dine inside of Chick-fil-A. My daughters love their Chick-fil-A sandwiches. It's something about a succulent, well- seasoned, juicy, fried chicken breast in between a toasted, buttery bun. The first bite is always accompanied by a mmm sound. Princess Armani took a big bite out of her sandwich and looked at me with a big smile as she continued to chew. After she took a big sip of her Sprite, she wiped her mouth and boldly said, "I bet you can make a chicken sandwich just as good as this!" I love the faith my children have in my cooking. But this statement put the pressure on me.

The very next day I went to the store to get the ingredients to make a chicken sandwich tasty enough to put that same smile on Princess Armani's face as her favorite Chick-fil-A sandwich did. Embarrassingly, I didn't get the same mmm as Chick-fil-A. So, I had to go back to the drawing board. I tweaked my recipe at least 7 times before my baby girl gave me the thumbs up! My husband always picks on me about how big the chicken breast is on the bun. But he always finishes every bite. Here's my Thicker Than Your Chick Sandwich.

Thicker Than Your Chick Sandwich

Ingredients

2 chicken breast (cut in half)
½ cup of (dill) pickle juice 2
eggs
¼ cup milk
1 cup flour
2 tablespoons powdered
sugar
2 tablespoons Tamika Scott's
"Poultry" Southern Fuse
4 buns
Peanut oil (for frying). Feel
free to fry it in canola oil if
there's peanut allergies.
Honey barbecue sauce
Pickle slices
Honey mustard

Directions

1. Inside of a large zip lock bag, pound chicken breast, with a meat tenderizer, until almost flat. Cut in half.
2. Marinade chicken breast in the pickle juice for 1 hour.
3. In a separate bowl, beat milk and egg. Put aside.
4. In a different bowl combine flour, sugar, and Poultry Fuse
5. Heat oil to 350°F. Dip chicken breast in the egg and milk mixture then coat in flour. Fry on each side 8-12 minutes, or until juices run clear when pierced with a fork. Drain on paper towel.
6. Toast bun, mix equal parts of honey barbecue sauce and honey mustard. Spread on bun, add pickle slice and garnish with your choice of tomatoes and lettuce.
7. Eat and enjoy!

Ingredients

For the chicken
4 small boneless and
skinless chicken breasts
2 tablespoons of vegetable oil
2 tablespoons of butter
Cooking spray
1 tablespoon of Tamika
Scott's "Poultry" Southern
Fuse."

For the salad
10 oz. leafy romaine lettuce
(or spinach)
¼ cup of ranch dressing (or
your favorite salad dressing
4 boiled eggs (peeled and
rinsed)
1 tablespoon of Tamika
Scott's "All-Purpose"
Southern Fuse
1 cup of mild cheddar
cheese shredded

Directions

1. Clean chicken and pat dry. Season both sides of the chicken breast with Poultry Fuse, set aside for 10 minutes.
2. In a skillet, over medium heat, add 1 tablespoon of vegetable oil and 1 tablespoon of butter. Make sure the oil coats the entire pan and is hot before adding the chicken.
3. Add two chicken breasts at a time. You don't want to overcrowd your skillet. Cook 7-8 minutes. Cover the skillet with a tightly fitted lid to keep the chicken moist. After 7-8 minutes, flip both chicken breasts over. Add 1 tablespoon of butter to the skillet. Swirl it around and cook chicken for 7-8 minutes on the other side. When done (make sure there's no pink in the middle), remove chicken. Set aside.
4. Add 1 tablespoon of vegetable oil to the pan again and 1 tablespoon of butter. Place the last two chicken breasts in a pan. Cover with lid and cook for 7-8 minutes. Flip chicken and cover again for another 7-8 minutes or until done. Take out of skillet set aside.
5. Cut boiled eggs in half and season with an "All-Purpose" Fuse on a separate plate.
6. In a large bowl, add leafy romaine lettuce. Sprinkle mild cheddar cheese on top.
7. Finally, add boiled eggs and chicken on top. Enjoy with your favorite salad dressing.

Armani's Orange Chickens

Ingredients

For Chicken
2 lbs. of boneless
chicken thighs (cut in
1inch cubes)
1 teaspoon of salt
1 teaspoon of white
pepper
1 cup of corn starch
3 cups of flour
1 large egg
1 ½ cups of water
2 tablespoons of
oil Oil for deep
fryer

Armani's Orange Sauce
1 teaspoon vegetable oil
½ teaspoon of fresh
ginger
1 tablespoon of fresh
garlic
¼ cup of granulated sugar
¼ cup brown sugar
¼ cup orange juice
¼ cup of vinegar
2 tablespoons of soy
sauce
2 tablespoons of water
2 tablespoons
cornstarch
1 teaspoon of sesame
oil

Directions

1. In a large bowl, combine flour, cornstarch, salt, and white pepper.
2. In the same bowl, add egg and stir. Mix in two and a half cups of water and stir. Next, add oil and stir until everything is incorporated.
3. Add chicken cubes to the mix. Cover and refrigerate for 30 minutes.
4. In a large skillet, over medium heat, add vegetable oil and garlic. Stir with a spatula for 30 seconds. Add orange juice, ginger, vinegar, granulated sugar, soy sauce, brown sugar, and stir.
5. Next, add sesame oil, two tablespoons of water, and 2tablespoons of cornstarch. Heat until orange sauce thickens.
6. Heat oil in deep-fryer to 350°F or a large frying pan to medium-high heat.
7. Take chicken out of the refrigerator, place a few at a time in the oil and fry 3- 5 minutes or until golden brown.
8. Add chicken to Armani's orange sauce coating for five minutes, occasionally stirring. Serve immediately.

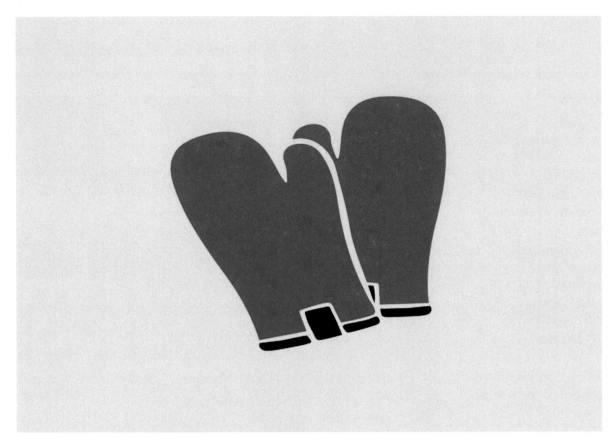

Daddy's Girl

Fishing was one of my favorite hobbies growing up. My father loved to fish, and I loved tagging along. His eyes would light up as he baited the fishing poles with slimy worms. I can't lie, sometimes that grossed me out, but as I grew older, baiting a fishhook became the norm. One day, my dad and I went fishing. He was talking as he was baiting the hook and accidentally put the point in his finger instead of the wiggly worm. He looked at me and didn't flitch. I knew he was in pain by the way he was breathing. He slowly took the hook out of his finger and applied pressure; he looked in his emergency kit, which he took with us everywhere we went and wrapped a Band-Aid around his wound. Afterward, he was ready to fish. I would've been prepared to go home after all of that pain. No, not my daddy. He was so tough and fearless!

Daddy never let anything stop him. Not even a hook penetrating through his finger. Unlike my dad, that day, I was lucky. I caught two big fish, and daddy let me reel them both in. Everyone came over to our area and watched as I reeled in the second fish. They were impressed to see a 9-year-old little girl handling a fishing pole as I did. My father brought a big round bucket with him to keep our caught fish in. That day, the only fish that was caught was my two-red snappers. Daddy was so proud of me but not as proud as I was of myself. I couldn't wait to get home and show my mother my big catch. When we arrived home, mom was on the phone in her room, which gave me enough time to get my fish ready for her to see.

They were a little muddy, so I took the bucket into my bathroom and ran cold water. I put them in one by one. They swam from one end of the tub to the next. I named them Peter and Billy. I was planning in my head where to put a fish tank in my room. My mom walked inside my bathroom and asked what I was doing. I moved away from the tub, and she let out a loud "what in the world!?!" I stood up proud and told her how I wanted to get a fish tank and keep them in my room. I told her the names I came up with and how I caught them on my own. Before she could begin fussing, my dad came inside and interrupted us by asking what we wanted for dinner. I told him hamburgers would be fine. He asked my mom to help him in the kitchen, leaving me alone with my two new friends. Minutes later, my mom told me she ran me bath water in her bathroom.

I told my fish goodbye, and I'd see them in a few. As I was bathing, my mom came in and read a good book to me. She even brought me a few of my barbie dolls to play with. I knew my mom was proud because she didn't rush me out of the tub like usual. But she did have to run more hot water because my water was now getting cold. A few minutes later, my sister, Latocha, came in and song us a new song she had written earlier that day. I loved to hear her sing. She had the most beautiful voice in the world. My mother and I clapped as she finished. Then we smelt a delicious aroma coming from the kitchen. My mom grabbed my towel and told me to get dressed because dinner was almost ready. My father made the best hamburgers ever! I was so hungry and couldn't wait to eat. After getting dressed, I ran to my bathroom to check on Peter and Billy, but they weren't there. I ran into the dining room, where my mom and sister were seated.   "Where's Peter and Billy?" I asked, concerned.

"Your father put them away." I looked down and saw the bucket they were in earlier. I didn't want to bother them until I finished eating, so I sat down at the dinner table. My dad walked out of the kitchen with his famous sweet hush puppies and his fried succulent shrimp. I was a little disappointed because I had a taste for his juicy hamburgers. I asked him if he'd take me shopping the next day to get a fish tank for my new fish. He didn't say a word. Instead, he walked back into the kitchen; this time, he came back with a plate with two pan-seared fish on it. I got up, ran, and opened the bucket only to see it was empty.

I took a deep breath, turned, and looked at my dad, who was looking at my mom. I walked back to the table with tears in my eyes. I sat down with my head hanging low. My father blessed the food, and I sat there. He told me that he took my fish out of the tub and put them in a big pan to put them in the bucket. He forgot that he left the water running in the kitchen, so he went straight there to cut the water off. He placed my fish on the side of the stove, where he had a pan getting hot for the shrimp and turned the water off. My fish jumped inside the pan and by the time he turned around, it was too late. They were already searing.

My father lowered his head, and I told him not to be sad because my fish was jumping inside the pan wasn1t his fault. I hugged him, and he said he was sorry. I felt better after that. In my 9-year-old mind, it wasn't his fault. My dad came home with a small fish tank with two tiny goldfish a few days later. As I grew older, I figured out what happened to Peter and Billy. And my father still has yet to confess.

Seared Snapping Red Snapper

Seared Snapping Red Snapper

Ingredients

(4) 6-8 oz. red snapper fillets
Tamika Scott's "Cajun" Southern Fuse
Olive oil cooking spray
2 tablespoons of avocado oil
1 lemon

Directions

1. Squeeze lemon juice on fillets, both sides.
2. Generously coat both sides of each fillet with Cajun Southern Fuse.
3. Spray both sides with olive oil cooking spray
4. Let sit for 20 minutes.
5. Heat 2 tablespoons of avocado oil in a large non-stick skillet or cast-iron skillet on medium-high heat. Make sure oil distributes evenly.
6. Allow the skillet to get hot.
7. Add fillets. Cook 4-5 minutes.
8. Carefully using a spatula, turn fish, and cook 4-5 minutes, or until fish is cooked thoroughly.
9. Carefully remove fish from pan to a serving plate.

Fried Succulent Shrimp

Ingredients

2 lbs. of raw shrimp, peeled, cleaned, deveined
1 ½ cup of all-purpose flour
½ cup of cornmeal
3 tablespoons of Tamika Scott's "Sea Food" Southern Fuse
2 tablespoons of "Tamika Scott's "Cajun" Southern Fuse
2 large eggs (beaten)
¼ cup of milk
1 tablespoon of hot sauce
3 cups of Canola Oil

Directions

1. Combine flour, cornmeal, 2 tablespoons of Cajun Fuse, and 2 tablespoons of Seafood Fuse in a large bowl.
2. In a small bowl, beat egg, then add milk, hot sauce, and one tablespoon of Seafood Fuse. Stir.
3. Heat oil over medium-high heat in a large skillet.
4. Dip shrimp in egg mixture, drip off excess egg mix.
5. Then dredge shrimp in the flour mix. Shake off excess flour. Lay shrimp on a serving plate and repeat the process for all shrimp.
6. Fry shrimp for 1-2 minutes on both sides or until golden brown.
7. Drain on a paper towel. And enjoy.

   I grew up in the '80s, where there was no compromising with children. What my parents said is what we did! No questions asked, no back talk, not even a funny face or frown made. My father was loving but militant! Everything we did had to be done meticulously; big or small! My sister and I had to hang the tissue over on the tissue roll. When using toothpaste, we squeezed from the bottom to the top. We weren't allowed to let the water run as we brushed our teeth, and you better wipe the sink dry and check the mirror to make sure nothing splashed on it. Yes, MILITANT! All the way down to what we ate.

   We could not drink our water until we were done eating—no elbows on the table, no talking with food in our mouths. Chew what's in your mouth at least ten times before swallowing to help your food digest properly. And most importantly, Eat All of Your Vegetables, if you like them or not. My sister liked everything. She never complained about the food, period! I would sit and stare at collard greens on my plate like it was the enemy. I despised the odorous aroma the collard greens produced while cooking! I had a master plan when it came down to eating them. I would inhale, then hold my breath before taking a bite. Then I'd breathe out of my mouth after I swallowed.

This method allowed me to avoid smelling and tasting this revolting vegetable until that one funny moment I would never forget. My father told a joke that was so hilarious, I forgot to hold my breath as I was swallowing a spoonful of collard greens. Hold up! Wait A Minute? That wasn't so bad. In fact, I actually liked the oniony flavor that lightly swept my tongue, followed by a kiss of heat from the red pepper flakes. All of the years I spent wasting energy holding my breath because I thought collards were nasty based on the smell (which is still not too pleasant today).

From that moment on, I vowed to myself to become acceptive to all foods. If I like it, I will eat it. If not, I'd spit it out. I went from despising collard greens to now being a cheerleader for this vitamin pack leafy, green vegetable. There are so many ways to cook them. They can be prepared the good old fashion southern way with onions, pork meat or Smoked Turkey wings, or no meat. You can make them in a soup or roll them up in a wrap, cook into a stir fry, or blend into a smoothie. However you decide to make them, is up to you. Today I'm going to share my Southern Style Collard Greens. I know you will enjoy it!

Mika's Southern Style Greens

Ingredients

3 bunches of fresh collard greens or 3 (16 oz) bags of collard greens)

1 whole smoked turkey wing, or 2 smoked turkey legs, or 2 Smoked ham hocks

2 large yellow onion (finely sliced)

1 tablespoon minced garlic

6 cups of chicken broth

1 tablespoon of sugar or agave

1½ tablespoon of distilled white vinegar

2½ tablespoons of hot sauce

4-6 tablespoons Tamika Scott's "Vegetable" Southern Fuse

½ lemon juice (to clean greens)

1 tablespoon of salt (to clean greens)

Directions

1. Tear the leaves from the stem or use kitchen scissors to cut leaves away from the stem. Fold leaves twice and cut to your desired size. Discard stems

2. Wash greens thoroughly, with warm water, ½ of lemon juice, and a tablespoon of salt. Then allow it to soak for a few minutes. Swish them around once again, then drain them in a large colander and rinse them again to make sure you feel no grit or see any dirt.

3. In a large pot, combine 1 ½ slice of onions and all ingredients (except collard greens) over medium heat. Stir and cover—Cook for 40 minutes. Turn pot to low.

4. Remove smoked turkey. Let cool. On the cutting board, cut smoke turkey meat into dice. Discard the bone.

5. Taste water to make sure the flavor is to your liking. Feel free to adjust the seasonings for your taste. Next, add half of the meat, then add collard greens, then the rest of the meat back to the pot.

6. Sprinkle a little Vegetable Fuse on top of collards. Add remaining onion slices. Cover with lid. Cook on low to medium heat for 1 hour or until greens have reached desired tenderness.

My daddy's sweet hush puppies were everyone's favorite! It was something about the sweet heat you would get from every bite. These were treats in our home growing up! Our parents only cooked bread on special occasions and we hardly ever ate sweets. Daddy made these if we were celebrating something special or if he'd upset my mom. He knew his famous hush puppies would make her forget whatever he did to make her mad.

Ingredients

1 cup of all-purpose flour
1 cup of cornmeal
1 tablespoons of baking powder
¼ cup of white sugar
1 tablespoon Tamika Scott's "All-Purpose" Southern Fuse
1 large egg beaten
1 cup of buttermilk
1 teaspoon of vegetable oil
1 can (14.75 oz.) cream-style sweet corn
1 teaspoon of jalapenos, chopped fine (optional)
2 qt. of vegetable oil (or oil of your choice)

Directions

1. Add (all dry ingredients) cornmeal, baking powder, sugar, All-purpose flour, fuse, jalapeno, and mix in a large bowl.
2. In a small bowl, whisk egg, then add milk.
3. Gradually combine egg and milk mixture with the dry mix in the large bowl while stirring.
4. Add cream corn and stir.
5. Let the mix sit for 8-10 minutes.
6. Heat oil in a large dutch oven or deep skillet to 330℉ (Cooking them too high will make them brown too fast because of the sugar).
7. Use your ice cream scooper or large spoon to scoop the mixture out. Drop into the oil.
8. Fry until golden brown, turning consistently for even cooking.
9. Drain on a paper towel and enjoy.

Not only did my dad make delicious, sweet hush puppies, he knew how to make the tastiest fried shrimp ever!

Check In!

Pause! Take a pic and let me see how your recipe came out. Tag me!

@TheRealTamikaScott
#CookingWithTamikaScott

Sister Friends are the Best Friends

When you think of Turkey, the first thing that comes to mind is Thanksgiving. I refuse to wait until Thanksgiving to eat some good ole turkey. My favorite part of the turkey are the wings, which are seasonal where I live. When I see them at the grocery store, I buy every pack I see. There are many ways to prepare them: grilling, frying, and slow cooking in the slow cooker with Cajun or lemon pepper seasoning. My favorite is baking them in the oven with sweet and smokey barbecue sauce. Talking about something good. Baby...Delicious is an understatement. I remember making them, and one of my best girlfriends, Cynthia, came over to visit. As soon as she walked in, she talked about how good the food smelled from outside the door. She couldn't wait to see what I cooked.

When she removed the foil from over the wings, she frowned and said, "What are these?" I told her, barbecue turkey wings. She frowned, "Barbecue? On turkey wings? Now sugar, youl're running out of things to cook!" I couldnl't wait to see what Cynthia's reaction would be after tasting them. I made her a small plate. She examined the meat covered in the sauce as if it was a pair of new shoes. Then she slowly put the fork to her mouth. Shortly afterward came, "I donl't know whether to kiss you or slap you! Girl, these wings are BANGING!" She continued to eat until she was licking her fingers. Ever since then, she knows not to sleep on any of my creations! All I hear her say now is, "Hurry up and finish your cookbook so I can get these recipes!" So here you are, Cynthia. And let me add; my "Southern Smothered Peas" and "Cajun Potato Salad" pair well with these Banging Turkey Wings.

Banging Barbecue Turkey Wings

Ingredients

3-4 whole turkey wings
1 yellow onion
2 tablespoons of Tamika Scott's "Poultry" Southern Fuse (to put in broth)
2 tablespoons of Tamika Scott's "Barbecue" Southern Fuse (to season wings)
1 (32oz) carton of turkey or chicken broth (enough to cover branches)
(Feel free to use your favorite barbecue sauce) or try mine.

Banging Barbecue Sauce
2½ cups of ketchup
3 teaspoons of liquid smoke
1 tablespoon of hot sauce
¼ cup Tamika Scott's "Sweetener" Southern Fuse
1 tablespoon of Tamika Scott's "Barbecue" Southern Fuse
2 tablespoons of Worcestershire sauce
1 tablespoon of maple syrup
1 tablespoon of Dijon mustard

Directions

1. Season both sides of turkey wings with "Poultry" Fuse. Set aside
2. In a large pot or dutch oven, add broth, onions, and 2 tablespoons "Barbecue" Fuse. Cover and bring to a boil.
3. Add wings and onions. Cover and cook on medium-high for 40 minutes.
4. Preheat oven to 350°F.
5. While turkey wings are boiling, prepare the Banging Sauce.
6. Over medium heat, in a large saucepan, combine all Banging Sauce ingredients. Stir and cover. Allow sauce to bubble. Uncover and stir. Turn on low and cover.
7. Skip steps 5 & 6 if you decide to use your favorite store-bought barbecue sauce.
8. Carefully transfer turkey wings only (no broth) to a large roasting pan or large baking dish.
9. Pour Banging Sauce on top of wings. Cover with foil and bake for 15 minutes.
10. Uncover wings and bake 20 minutes or to your desired crispiness.

Ingredients

2 teaspoons butter
2 tablespoons butter
1 cup minced white onions
21 tablespoon Tamika Scott's "Vegetable" Southern Fuse
32 tablespoons all-purpose flour
4 cups whole milk
4 cups sweet green peas, blanched and drained (about 1 1/2 lbs. frozen peas)
1/2 cup breadcrumbs
2 oz. grated mild cheddar cheese
2 oz. grated parmesan cheese

Directions

1. Preheat the oven to 400°F. Grease an 8-cup oval or square glass dish with two teaspoons of the butter and set aside.
2. In a large sauté pan, over medium-high heat, melt the remaining two tablespoons of butter. Add the onions and season with Vegetable Fuse, sauté for 2 minutes. Add the flour and cook for 1 minute, stirring constantly.
3. Stir in the milk and bring the mixture to a simmer. Cook for 4 to 6 minutes or until the mixture is thick enough to coat the back of a spoon. Add the peas and mix thoroughly, then pour into the prepared pan.
4. Sprinkle breadcrumbs over the peas and top with the grated cheese.
5. Place the pan in the oven and bake until bubbly and the top is lightly golden, about 10 to 12 minutes.
6. Remove the pan from the oven and serve.

Ingredients

3 lbs. of potatoes
1 small Vidalia onion (chopped)
1 cup Miracle Whip or Duke mayo
1 tablespoon Dijon mustard
¼ cup sweet pickles
2 teaspoons sugar
31 tablespoon of salt
2 tablespoon Tamika Scott's "Cajun" Southern Fuse
6 hardboiled eggs (shelled & diced) for potato salad
6 hardboiled eggs (shelled & chopped) for garnishing

Directions

1. Peel, cut, and cube potatoes, place them in a large stock pot, cover with cold water, and bring them to a boil. Once boiling, add salt and cook the potatoes for 15-20 minutes, until fork tender.
2. Fill a saucepan about a quarter of the way with cold water. Place the eggs in a single layer at the bottom of the saucepan. Add more water so that the eggs are covered by at least an inch or two of water.
3. Heat the pot on high heat and bring the water to a full boil. You can add a teaspoon of vinegar to the water to help keep egg whites from running out of egg cracks while cooking. Adding 1/2 teaspoon of salt to the water helps prevent cracking and makes the eggs easier to peel.
4. Turn off the heat, keep the pan on the burner, cover, and let sit for 10-12 minutes. Strain the water from the pan and run cold water over the eggs to cool them quickly and stop them from cooking further. I like to peel them under the running water. After peeling, dice the eggs.
5. Mix miracle whip, Vidalia onion, dijon mustard, sweet pickles, sugar, and Cajun Fuse in a medium bowl. Add in potatoes and eggs, stir until blended well.
6. Cover the Cajun potato salad and refrigerate for at least 4 hours. It tastes even better the next day!

I often tell people I'm on a diet, and when they ask me what kind of diet, I tell them a seafood diet because I eat what I see. Bahahaha. I laugh at that joke every time I say it. Seafood is my ultimate favorite food of all time. If I had a choice to eat only one type of food for a year, it would be Seafood! I grew up eating all kinds of seafood; shark meat, shrimp, lobster, octopus, crab legs, all types of fish, and I can't forget frog legs. Hold up; frog legs aren't seafood. But they are mmm, mmm good! So yes, I love some seafood, but I also enjoy Italian as well. When you put them together, you get my Sea-Talian Lasagna!

There's something about layers of creaminess on top of a seafood medley swimming in a bed of spinach covered in cheese. I can hear music coming from my oven like a classical orchestra accompanied by a DJ in the background scratching on turntables. I love watching the cheese melt on top of the noodles! I stand and stare in front of the oven like a puppy looking out of the window, waiting for its owner to come home.

Ingredients

1 lb. of lasagna noodles

2 lbs. of medium shrimp, peeled, deveined, uncooked

(2) 8oz lump crab meat (or less expensive imitation)

2 tablespoons of cooking olive oil

4 tablespoons of butter

1 large egg

3 teaspoons of minced garlic

2¼ cups of ricotta cheese

(1) 16oz of fresh baby spinach (chopped)

2 tablespoon of Tamika Scott's "Seafood" Southern Fuse (for shrimp)

3 tablespoons of Tamika Scott's "All-Purpose" Southern Fuse (for noodles)

4 tablespoons of Tamika Scott's "Cajun" Southern Fuse (for sauce)

3 cups of heavy whipping cream

½ cup of milk

2 tablespoons all-purpose flour

3 cups of Kraft creamy melt mozzarella cheese shredded

2 cups of freshly grated parmesan cheese

(2) 32 oz. seafood broth

(1) 32 oz. chicken broth

Salt and pepper to taste (for noodles)

Directions

1. Preheat oven to 350°F.
2. Bring seafood broth, chicken broth, salt, pepper, and 3 tablespoons of All-Purpose Fuse in a large pot to a boil. Add cooking oil. Make sure broth is boiling before adding lasagna noodles. Cook noodles al dente, noodles still firm and not cooked all the way. Lay noodles flat on a greased baking sheet.
3. In a medium bowl, combine shrimp (cut in half) and crab meat. Season with 1 tablespoon of Seafood Fuse. Set aside.
4. In a medium bowl, mix ricotta cheese, baby spinach, egg, and 1 cup of parmesan—season with 1 tablespoon of Seafood Fuse.
5. In a medium pot, over medium-high heat, melt 2 tablespoons of butter. Add minced garlic and stir for 25 seconds. Whisk in milk and flour for 1 minute. Whisk in heavy whipping cream. Whisk well—season with Cajun Fuse and mix. Cover and bring to a simmer, stirring occasionally, and cook until sauce thickens. Stir in 1 cup of parmesan cheese. Turn off heat. Remove pot from the burner.
6. In a large baking dish, spread a thin layer of sauce from the pot on the bottom of the pan. Next, lay noodles on top—spread ricotta and spinach mixture on top of noodles. Now, add a layer of shrimp and crab meat on top of the spinach mixture. Next, cover with sauce and sprinkle with mozzarella cheese.
7. Repeat for three more layers, ending with mozzarella on top.
8. Carefully cover the lasagna with foil. Bake 50 minutes. Remove foil and bake 10 minutes more or until cheese is golden and completely melted. Allow sitting 15 minutes before serving. Sprinkle Cajun Fuse on top for a delicious garnish.

When I was a little girl, my mother always rewarded me with one starch, of course after I ate my vegetables. Macaroni and cheese was and is my absolute favorite. I loved the creaminess of the cheese that dressed each noodle. It was something about the sharpness of the cheddar in every bite. Now, as an adult, I still reward myself with this delicious comfort food.

I guess I passed the "I Love Macaroni and Cheese" trait down to my kids and Glam-Babies. I find myself telling them the same thing my mom told me as a little girl, "eat your vegetables, then you can eat your mac and cheese." Somehow that doesn't work for me. My Glam-Baby, Aveyah, looks up at me and stuffs multiple noodles in her mouth. Shortly after, she began smacking, and umm sound followed after each bite. I'm either getting older or soft because I never fuss. To make it a little healthier, I added spinach to my macaroni. I didn't think the kids would like it, but I tried it anyway. Aveyah frowned after she saw the wilted green spinach peeking through the cheese. I took a bite and pretended it was the best thing I'd ever tasted. My Glam-Baby watched as I rubbed my belly, making a delicious sound with my eyes closed. She looked at her spoon, smelled the mac and cheese, and frowned again. Oh well, there goes that idea. Then suddenly, she took a bite and mimicked exactly what I did but with a frown on her face. Surprisingly, she took another bite and another, smacking in between each bite. I watched with a smile and couldn't believe my idea worked. Now I don't have to feel guilty because they are eating their vegetables with my Smack'N Mac'N Cheese.

Smack' N' Mac' N Cheese

Ingredients

1 (16) oz. box of elbow noodles
2 cups of fresh baby spinach
3 cup of Creamy Melt Mozzarella
4 cups of Creamy Melt Triple Cheddar
1 cup of Creamy Melt Sharp Cheddar
1 cup of Creamy Melt Mexican Style
2 cups of Creamy Triple Cheddar (Topping)
2 cups of milk
2 cups of whipping cream
5 cups of chicken broth
2 large eggs
2 tablespoons of cooking oil
3 tablespoons of Tamika Scott's "All-Purpose" Southern Fuse
2 tablespoons of "Tamika Scott's "Vegetable" Southern Fuse
1 tablespoon of black pepper (for boiling noodles)
1 tablespoon of black pepper (when mixing with cheese)

Directions

1. In a large pot, add chicken broth, All-Purpose Fuse, and black pepper. Bring to a boil.
2. Add cooking oil to broth, bring back to a boil.
3. Preheat oven to 350°F.
4. Add noodles to boiling water. Cook 10 minutes or until a little under al dente.
5. After noodles are done (and still firm), drain and set aside.
6. Add noodles to a large bowl. In the same bowl, combine noodles, milk, cheese (except triple cheddar), whipping cream, Vegetable Fuse, black pepper, and stir. Make sure your cheese mixture is well distributed throughout the macaroni.
7. Add spinach and eggs. Stir.
8. Evenly pour Smack'N Mac'N Cheese in an oven-proof, greased baking dish.
9. Cook in the oven for 30 minutes. Remove mac and cheese from the oven. Top off with Triple Cheddar. Cook for 7-8 more minutes or until cheese is completely melted

I was a freshman in high school and started dating a guy a year older than me. Every day we talked on the phone and he would be eating a hamburger. That was his absolute favorite food. I made up my mind that the next time he came to my house to visit me, I would surprise him and cook the juiciest hamburger he had ever tasted. I was always taught, the way to a man's heart is through his stomach, and I wanted to make a great impression on him. Twenty minutes before he was to arrive at my house, I looked in the freezer to get out a few burger patties, but to my surprise, they were all gone.

Thankfully, my mom left ground beef in the fridge to make spaghetti when she got off from work. I had a plan; I would make burgers instead, and she would be surprised as well. Then all of a sudden, it dawned on me that I never made hamburgers using ground beef, only the frozen patty ones. How hard could it be? I've seen my mom make them a million times. She seasoned the beef, rolled them in a big ball, and pat them out. I just couldn't remember if she made them on top of the stove or in the oven. So, I decided to put them in the oven. I set the temperature to 350 degrees Fahrenheit, put them on a baking pan, and closed the oven. Minutes later, my boyfriend arrived. I hurried up and put on my mother's kitchen apron, then I let him in.

"It smells good in here! Are you cooking?" He asked as he came through the door. I tried to play it down and told him I threw something together. He gave me the biggest hug and kiss. I was trying to hold back my blush and keep a straight face. I told him the food I put in the oven would be done in a minute and to have a seat. As we waited, I pulled out a pack of orange Kool-Aid. I grabbed two oranges and cut them up while we spoke. He was so impressed! My mission was being accomplished. He complimented me and told me how cute I looked in my apron and how special he felt that I cooked something for him. He grabbed my hand and kissed it while telling me that no other girlfriend had ever cooked for him before.

After silently screaming with joy inside of my head, I poured him some of my delicious Kool-Aid. Yes, it was the bomb! I told him the food should be ready now. He volunteered to take it out of the oven. I sat as he grabbed the kitchen mittens to retrieve my surprise. After opening up the oven, he let out a loud, "oh my gosh, I love these." My smile turned upside down as soon as I heard him say, "Italian Meatballs." What? As soon as he turned towards me, I saw what was supposed to be juicy plump hamburgers had now shrunk down to itty bitty meatballs. OMG. What did I do wrong? I couldn't tell him they were supposed to be hamburgers, and I couldn't panic. Especially after all the nice compliments he gave me just a few minutes earlier. So, I did the next best thing. I took the spaghetti sauce my mom left out and warmed it up a little in the microwave.

I took the hamburger buns, added cheese, and drizzled the spaghetti sauce on top of the meatballs, and made him a meatball sandwich. He was even more impressed. He had never had a meatball sandwich before (neither had I), and he said it was one of the best things he'd ever eaten! A few years later, I got an engagement ring that I should've turned down. Maybe I should've told him the truth and saved me ten years of my life... Some people are just meant to be friends!

Ingredients

4 Hoagie rolls
1 lb. of ground beef OR 1 lb.
ground beef & ½ lb. of ground
pork
1 cup of Italian style
breadcrumbs
½ cup of (fresh grated)
parmesan cheese
2 large eggs
½ cup of water
½ cup of ricotta cheese
1 ½ tablespoon of Tamika
Scotts "Beef" Southern Fuse
1 teaspoon of minced garlic
1 jar of Marinara sauce (use
your favorite store- brought
sauce)

Directions

1. Preheat oven to 350°F. Prepare meatballs for the oven.
2. In a large bowl, mix 1lb of ground beef with breadcrumbs, parmesan, ricotta cheese, eggs, minced garlic, and "Beef" Fuse. Use your clean hands to mix, adding water gradually. Until mixed thoroughly.
3. Roll mixture into a perfect ball and place them in oven baking dish. You can roll them in large balls or medium size.
4. Bake 10 minutes, turn, and bake for eight more minutes or until golden brown.
5. In a medium saucepan, warm up the marinara sauce.
6. Place two meatballs on a Hoagie roll, drizzle marinara on top of the meat.
7. Garnish with your choice of lettuce, cheese, or jalapeños.

My family has so much love and admiration for one another that when we don't understand each other's views on a particular matter, we respectfully agree to disagree. We pray together, eat together, and at times, we work together. There's so much peace in our home... until Football Season! We all have our favorite teams we root for. My husband is a Steelers Fan, my mom's a Falcon Fan, my daughter is a Cowboys fan, and I often root for the underdogs. It gets really intense in our home at game time. You can hear us screaming and rooting for our favorite teams a mile away. We make jokes and smack talk each other until the game is over and at the end of the game, the person whose team wins brags for the rest of the day. We can never agree on what team is the best, but the one thing we do agree on, is my Slam'n Philly Cheese Sliders. These bite-size melted cheese, beefy delights are sure to score a touchdown every time!

Tamika's Slam'n Philly Sliders

Ingredients

12 Hawaiian slider rolls

1 lb. thinly sliced ribeye steak

1 medium onion (thinly sliced)

1 green pepper (thinly sliced)

4 oz. mushrooms (sliced)

7 slices of provolone cheese

½ cup shredded Mozzarella Creamy Melt Cheese

¾ teaspoon Tamika Scott's "Beef" Southern Fuse

¾ teaspoon Tamika Scott's "Vegetable" Southern Fuse

2 tablespoons oil

Garlic butter (to spread on top of rolls)

Directions

1. In a large skillet over medium-high heat, add oil, bell peppers, onions, mushrooms, and steak. Sprinkle Beef Fuse and Vegetable Fuse on top of meat and vegetables and stir. Cook 8 minutes or until your desired doneness.
2. Preheat oven to 350°F. Line a baking pan with aluminum foil.
3. Slice the Hawaiian rolls in half through the middle. Place the bottom half of the roll in the baking pan. Spread garlic butter evenly on top rolls.
4. Place provolone cheese on bread in a baking pan. Layer the steak mixture on top of the provolone cheese.
5. Sprinkle Mozzarella Creamy Melt Cheese on top of steak mixture. Place top layer roll on and cover with foil. Cook 10 minutes, remove the foil, and cook 6-8 more minutes or until cheese completely melts and rolls are golden brown. Enjoy immediately.

Check In!

Pause! Take a pic and let me see how your recipe came out. Tag me!

@TheRealTamikaScott
#CookingWithTamikaScott

A Mother's Love

Oshun is my oldest daughter. I was 7 ½ months pregnant with her in X-scape's music video, "Love on My Mind." It's 28 years later, and she thinks she is my mother. Oshun is so sweet and yet stern at times. She's a little more serious than I am and will get you all the way together. I have to save my glam-babies when she fusses at them. Especially my three-year-old glam-baby, Aveyah. The other day when I went to my daughter's house, Oshun chastised Aveyah for not listening to her. All of a sudden, Aveyah started screaming and crying, "Glam-Ma!" My daughter was strict with Aveyah, telling her to go to her room until she calmed down. I felt so bad. I wanted to grab her and run out of the door. I turned and walked away.

It broke my heart hearing her cry all the way up the stairs. Oshun turned and looked at me to see if I would follow her. Instead, I walked into the kitchen to make myself a plate of Oshun's famous buffalo chicken dip she had just made. As I began washing my hands, Oshun went into the restroom. I quickly dried them and ran as fast as I could up the stairs. Aveyah was lying on her bed when I walked in. Before I could pick her up to give her a hug, Oshun yelled up the steps, "Momma, Come Back Down Here Right Now, And Leave Her Alone!" Aveyah looked at me as if I was getting into trouble, so I yelled back down the stairs, "Whom Do You Think You're Talking To Like That! I Am Your Mother!"

Aveyah looked at me and gave me the biggest smile. She was happy to see her mom getting fussed at. Then she gave me a kiss and said, "It's ok, Glam-Ma, don't be mad." Then we began to hug until we looked up and saw my daughter standing in the doorway to Aveyah's bedroom. Our hug stopped abruptly until Aveyah said, "uh-oh!" Then after a few seconds of silence, we all started to laugh.

Oshun's Buffalo Chicken Dip

Oshun's Buffalo Chicken Dip

Ingredients

2 cups rotisserie chicken (cooked and shredded)
6 oz. cream cheese (room temperature and softened)
½ cup hot sauce
½ cup ranch dressing
1 cup mild cheddar cheese (mix in)
½ cup Mexican style shredded cheese (topping)
1 teaspoon of Tamika Scott's "All-Purpose" Southern Fuse

Directions

1. Preheat oven to 350°F. In a medium bowl, combine sour cream chicken, All-purpose Fuse, hot sauce, ranch dressing, and mild cheddar cheese. Mix until well incorporated.
2. Spread into a greased casserole baking dish. Cook for 16 minutes.
3. Remove from oven and top with Mexican-style cheese. Bake for 5 minutes or until cheese completely melts on top.
4. Serve with tortilla chips.

Oshun's Mozzarella Cheese Sticks

Ingredients

16 creamy mozzarella string cheese sticks
1 ½ cup Italian style breadcrumbs
⅓ cup all-purpose flour
1 teaspoon of Tamika Scott's "All-Purpose" Southern Fuse
2 eggs
2 teaspoons milk
Oil for frying
1 cup of marinara sauce (for dipping)

Directions

1. Freeze string cheese overnight or 5 hours prior to cooking. If overnight, take it out of the freezer right before making it.
2. Place Italian crumbs in a medium-sized bowl. Place flour and All-Purpose Fuse in a small bowl. Mix to incorporate.
3. Place milk and eggs in a small bowl and beat until well mixed.
4. Dip each piece of cheese into flour, then into egg mix, followed by the breadcrumbs. Place each finished piece on a sheet pan lined with parchment paper.
5. Repeat until all cheese has been coated.
6. Heat oil in a deep pan to 350°F.
7. Place a few cheese sticks in the pan at a time. Cook 2-3 minutes on both sides or until golden brown.
8. Drain the cheese sticks on a paper towel. Serve with marinara sauce and enjoy.

Is That Legal Fruit Salad

My husband watched my mom prepare her salad when we went to an all you can eat establishment in disbelief. Her plate was piled high with everything possible that you could put in a salad. My husband looked at me and jokingly whispered, "Is that legal?" I laughed watching my mom walk around the salad bar carefully, like a lioness sneaking up on her prey, making sure not to forget anything. Then she proudly pranced back to the table as if she was holding an Academy Award. I can't begin to tell you what was all on her salad. My laughter stopped abruptly as soon as I thought about what he would think about me as soon as he saw my salad. Before I got up from the table, I told him to not say a word or think about judging my plate, (which wouldn't be nearly as devastating as my mom's)! Guess what? He did, but I didn't care. As a matter of fact, I got him to taste it and he loved it. Now he's hooked. Got Him! He learned a very valuable lesson that day. Never judge a salad by its content. Here's my "Is That Legal?" Fruit Salad. Feel free to add anything you'd like to this recipe.

Is That Legal Fruit Salad

Ingredients

1 bag of lettuce (or fresh at the farmers market)
3 mandarins (peeled and sliced)
3 cups of raisins
3 cups of strawberries halved
3 cups of seedless grapes
2 cups of fetta cheese
Salad dressing of your choice

Directions

1. Arrange lettuce in a medium bowl.
2. Add mandarins, strawberries, grapes, fetta cheese and raisins.
3. Drizzle with your favorite salad dressing.

My mother always gets on me about not watching the news like I should. I not only pass up on the news, but I don't watch TV at all as I stated in the beginning. Every now and then, at least once a month, my family and I will sit down in the theater room and watch a good movie. I'm guilty to say, the entire time the movie is on, I'm thinking about what I could be doing creatively or what chores I should be doing around the house. Watching the news makes you paranoid or depressed. There's never anything positive on. So, I stopped watching the news altogether. My mom calls me every day and tells me what the temperature will be or what is going on around my neighborhood. She is my weather forecaster, detective, political adviser, and the global informant.

Who needs TV when you have Mama Gloria Action News? On this particular day, my mother called to inform me that it was going to snow. What???!!! SNOW?? We live in Georgia, where our winters are some statesl summers, and it's going to snow? My mom told me to make sure we had all of the essentials because she didn't want me getting out to drive anywhere after the snows falls. First of all, I am embarrassed to say that "EVERYTHING" in the State of Georgia shuts down when we even think it may snow. Most of the time its only one to two inches, and we celebrate like we're about to go skiing in the Colorado Mountains. My husband always laughs at the way we react to snow. He was born and raised in New York City where the kids continue to go to school in six feet of snow. In Georgia, things are a lot different.

After receiving my mother's panicking news, I looked in my pantry to see what I would need from the store. Needless to say, I didn't need anything. I saw a few cans of black beans and kidney beans, a bag of Chili Cheese Frito Corn Chips, and a pack of Chili-O Seasoning so I knew exactly what I was going to make. My Quick Beefy Chili. This will last a day or two (which is even better the next day) and my family can't get enough of this delicious classic.

For long days at home due to the weather or busy days, there is nothing like a slow cooker. The best thing about a slow cooker is the fact you can put whatever you're cooking inside, season it, turn it on, cover it up, and go by your merry little way. You can run an errand, clean your house, do some work on the computer, or even lay down and relax. I love how the slow cooker intensifies the flavors in my Pot Roast and how it tenderizes it to perfection. Plus, the slow cooker uses less electricity than an electric or gas oven. There are so many things I enjoy putting in my slow cooker, like my roast beef and vegetables, my turkey wings, oxtails, neckbones, meatballs, and the list goes on. Everything I cook in it is definitely a crowd-pleaser!

Tamika's Quick Meaty Chili

Ingredients

2 Packs (2.25 oz.) French's Chili-O Seasoning Mix with Onions

2 lbs. of ground beef

1 lb. of Italian sausage (Mild, casings removed)

1 Can (16oz) dark red kidney beans, drained

1 Can (16oz) Black Beans, drained

2 cans (14.5oz) diced tomatoes, with juice

1 can (6oz) Tomato Paste

Optional for topping: Sour cream, shredded mild cheddar cheese

1 Large yellow onion diced

Directions

1. Over medium high heat, In a large skillet, brown ground beef and sausage. add onions 3 minutes into browning. Drain fat.

2. Add all ingredients to slow cooker and stir. cook on high for 3 hours. Taste to make sure seasoning is to your liking. Feel free to add salt and pepper or hot sauce for extra flavor.

3. Cover and cook 1 hour. If desired add sour cream and shredded cheese for garnishing.

Mika's Slow-Cooked Pot Roast with Vegetables

Ingredients

1 (3 to 5 lbs.) boneless beef chuck roast
1 tablespoon of canola oil
2 cups of beef broth
1 cups of dry red wine
2 packets Lipton Beefy Onion Soup Mix
1 tablespoon of brown sugar
1 tablespoon Worcestershire Sauce
3 garlic cloves (minced)
1 large onion, halved and sliced
1 medium green pepper, halved and sliced
2 celery ribs, chopped
3 tablespoon of black pepper
4 teaspoons of sea salt
53 potatoes (peeled and quartered)
6 cups carrots (cut into 2-inch chunks)

Directions

1. Drizzle olive oil into a large pan or dutch oven over medium-high heat.
2. Sprinkle additional sea salt and black pepper on both sides of the roast.
3. Then add roast and sear on each side for 3-4 minutes.
4. Carefully remove roast and place it aside.
5. Add beef broth, red wine, brown sugar, sea salt, black pepper, Worcestershire Sauce, onions, one pack of Beefy Lipton Soup Mix, and garlic to slow cooker (stir)
6. Add Roast.
7. In a medium bowl or cup, add 1 pack of beefy soup mix with a half cup of water. Mix together and pour on top of the roast.
8. Cover and cook for 4 hours on a medium to high setting.
9. Add celery, carrots, and potatoes. Cover and cook for 4-5 more hours, or until desired tenderness

My fashionista mother-in-love, Mrs. Georgia, better known as "Gi-Gi," be dressing her behind off! Everything matches from head to her toe. She never wears the same thing twice and she always shows up, to show out! Not only in her fashion but also in the kitchen. Every time she comes over, we request her New York Fried Chicken. When I tell you, "The Colonel" doesn't have anything on my My Mother in Love, please believe it! Her chicken is so good I've seen people burn their tongues, eating it straight out of the grease. Gi-Gi isn't your average cook. She does things her way. I watch her as she cleans the chicken. She always explains what she's doing as if she's on a cooking show. I always laugh to myself, but I give her my undivided attention.

"Look Here, you have to make sure there are no feathers attached to the skin." Then she scrubs that same chicken wing for ten minutes. By the time she cooks the chicken, itls barely anything left on it. Hahahahaha, I'm just kidding, but it is squeaky clean. I make sure to have everything she needs to cook her chicken the way she likes to—all the way down to the hot sauce. If I didn't, I would hear her complain the entire time we eat. So, I always keep a stash of her preferred hot sauce in my spice cabinet. Between laughing and talking on the phone to explaining how to cook step by step, my mother-in love always keeps me entertained. She never disappoints with her New York Fried Chicken, and there are never any leftovers.

Gigi's Fried Chicken

Ingredients

10 pieces chicken (I prefer wings, but it's your preference)

3 - 4 tablespoons Tamika Scott's "Poultry" Southern Fuse

1 qt. vegetable, canola, or peanut oil for frying

2 cups hot sauce

1 ½ tablespoon Tamika Scott's "All-Purpose" Southern Fuse Seasoned Flour

3 cups all-purpose flour

¼ cup cornstarch

6 - 8 tablespoons Tamika Scott's "Poultry" Southern Fuse

Directions

1. Season chicken with Tamika Scott's "All-Purpose" Southern Fuse and "Poultry Fuse." Add hot sauce on both sides of the chicken. Set aside.

2. Combine flour, cornstarch, Poultry Fuse together in a gallon-sized resealable bag/paper bag or large shallow bowl and shake or whisk to combine it well.

3. After the chicken has marinated, add oil to a heavy-bottomed skillet, cast iron, deep fryer, or dutch oven until it's about 1-2 inches deep—heat oil to 350°F.

4. Remove chicken pieces from hot sauce marinade, shaking to remove excess marinade. Add to seasoned flour mixture, coating well. Shake gently to remove excess flour.

5. Place chicken in hot oil; try not to overcrowd them for best results.

6. Fry chicken 14-16 minutes, turning chicken over or occasionally shaking basket if using a deep fryer. Remove chicken pieces from oil and place them on a baking sheet lined with paper towels or a wire rack.

7. Let the chicken rest 5-10 minutes before serving. Enjoy the chicken with your favorite sides.

*Note, if you're new to frying chicken, having a thermometer is your best friend. Chicken is done when it reaches an internal temperature of at least 165°F.

I come from a big family. My great-grandmother had fifteen children and my grandmother had ten of her own. Five boys and five girls. My Aunt Della was the 2nd child to be born out of the ten and she is a force to be reckoned with. I spent a lot of time with my aunt in my middle school days. She would do hair from her home and always found time to cook in between. After relaxing my hair bone straight and styling it to the gauds, she washed her hands and hurried into the kitchen to check on her roast in the oven. As soon as she opened the oven this delicious, mesmerizing fragrance swept through my nostrils. "I have 20 minutes before my next client will be here."

I watched as she pulled her green peppers, onions, cabbage, and bacon out of the refrigerator. I quickly frowned as she began to cut up her vegetables. The onions teared my eyes. After seeing me wipe the tears away, she turned on the cold water to rinse the onion. My aunt explained to me that my eyes were tearing because of the gases being released and running the onion under cold water will allow the fumes to be rinsed off. I didn't like onions, or cabbage so I wasn't interested in her tutorial. I didn't want to hurt my aunt's feelings, so I continued to listen as she prepared her cabbage. She started off frying the bacon which made me hungry for breakfast.

Then she added in the green peppers and onions. The redolence of scents in the pan made my stomach growl. I went from not being interested to now wanting to taste the finished product. Aunt Della added the cabbage and covered her pot. Fifteen minutes later, it was done. My aunt put a small amount on a little saucer. I blew the smoke off of the cabbage and took a bite. OMG!!!! I never knew cabbage could be so good. From that very moment I was hooked and couldn't wait for my mom (Who had to whip me to eat her cabbages) to come pick me up so I could get my Aunt Della to teach her how to make cabbage the way she did. Through the years I have made a few adjustments to the ingredients. And you can best believe it's not your average cabbage!

Ingredients

1 medium head of cabbage (washed and sliced)

1 green bell pepper (Thinly sliced)

1 red pepper (Thinly sliced)

1 white onion (Thinly sliced) 2 cups of chicken or turkey broth

1 tablespoon of hot sauce (0r ¼ teaspoon of red pepper flakes for more heat)

1 teaspoon black pepper

1 teaspoon Tamika Scott's All-Purpose Southern Fuse

1 smoked turkey wing

3 tablespoon of Tamika Scott's Vegetable Southern Fuse

Directions

1. Bring broth, smoked turkey wing, salt, pepper, garlic powder, Tamika Scott's "Vegetable" Southern Fuse, and hot sauce to a boil.

2. Add green pepper, red pepper, and onions to broth. Simmer for 2 minutes.

3. Add cabbage, sprinkle with 1 tablespoon Tamika Scottl s "Vegetable" Southern Fuse and cover. Simmer for 10 minutes.

4. Stir and cover. Simmer for 2-4 more minutes, or until desired tenderness.

Foods That Gets You In The Mood

I am a romantic being who loves, love! Yes, probably the most affectionate person I know! When communicating, I like to look directly into one's eyes. There's a saying; your eyes are the windows to your soul. I can feel a person's vulnerability, shyness, insecurities, concerns, and strengths just by sincere eye contact.

Every time I look into my husband's eyes, I know if he wants affection, love, or just wants to be sexed. I can also feel and see the love he has for me. I dedicate this section of recipes as my Love Foods. Food can be sexy, and it can also put you in the mood. Here are my choices when I want to be a little more romantic.

Watermelon

Don't let this sweet fruit fool you. Watermelon helps stimulate the release of nitric oxide in your body. Nitric oxide allows oxygen, nutrients, and blood to flow effectively throughout every part of your beautiful body. Watermelon contains an amino acid, that helps things get up and stay up. Not only does it increase blood flow, but it also lowers blood pressure. So, here's my go-to adult watermelon delight. It's guaranteed to get you in the mood.

Sexy-Melon-Jell-O-Shots

Ingredients

*Half of a medium
seedless
watermelon
(1) 1 oz. box of Knox
unflavored gelatin (4
envelopes inside)
(2)3 oz. boxes of
watermelon flavored
Jell-O
1 cup of water
1½ cup of juice from
the watermelon
1½ cup of watermelon
flavored vodka (or
vodka of your choice)
Granulated sugar
(optional)
Ice cream scooper
or considerable
spoon*

Directions

1. Use your ice cream scooper or large spoon to scoop the pink watermelon flesh out of the watermelon. Leave the white of the rind.
2. Drain all of the juice from the watermelon in a large bowl and set it aside.
3. Cut 2 cups of watermelon into small cubes, sprinkle with sugar, and set aside.
4. Place the hollowed-out watermelon rind in the freezer while you prepare the Jell-O
5. In a medium saucepan, bring 1 cup of water and 1 cup of watermelon juice to a boil
6. Add the Knox unflavored gelatin (all four envelopes) with the two watermelon boxes to the boiling water, one pack at a time. Whisk together until powder COMPLETELY dissolves in the water. Once dissolved, allow the mixture to sit and cool down. (Making sure the mix is cooled before adding vodka is very important. Adding vodka to the boiling mixer burns off the alcohol, and you don't want that to happen.)
7. Once the mixer is cooled down, whisk well to ensure that all parts are dissolved. Next, add 1½ cups of watermelon vodka and ½ cup of watermelon juice.
8. Take watermelon rind out of the freezer.
9. Add watermelon cubes inside the halved watermelon rind.
10. Pour liquid inside of watermelon on top of the fruit.
11. Gently mix fruit evenly around
12. Carefully place your watermelon (try not to spill) in the refrigerator for 4-5 hours, or until Jell-O is firm and set
13. When ready to serve, take watermelon out of the refrigerator, cut off any excess rind. Slice it with a large knife in the sizes that you like and enjoy. Be sure to keep watermelon slices cold in the refrigerator when not serving.

Spinach

This green leafy vegetable is a beautiful energy food. The magnesium in it also helps with the blood flow to the genitals, increasing arousal in both women and men. This is one of the best foods for stamina. Try my Skinny Dipping Spinach for a hot date night.

Ingredients

1lb. fresh baby spinach
1 ½ tablespoon olive or avocado oil
¼ cup finely chopped onion
1 tablespoon minced garlic
3 mushroom caps (chopped)
1 teaspoon Tamika Scott's "Vegetable" Southern Fuse
½ Teaspoon Tamika Scott's "All-Purpose" Southern Fuse 1 teaspoon freshly squeezed lemon juice (optional but tasty)

Directions

1. In a large dutch oven pot, heat oil over medium heat
2. Add onions and sauté for 2 minutes.
3. Add mushrooms and sauté for 2 minutes.
4. Add minced garlic and stir for 1 minute.
5. Add Spinach, Vegetable Fuse, All-Purpose Fuse, and stir to mix seasonings in and coat spinach in oil. Cook 4 minutes or until spinach is wilted.
6. After 4 minutes, stir and remove from heat. Add lemon juice and stir.
7. Transfer to serving dish with a slotted spoon to drain the juice.

Skinny Dipping Spinach

Ingredients

Bag of tortilla chips 20 oz.
frozen spinach (thawed
and drained)
¼ cup of chicken broth
¼ cup of flour
1 tablespoon of minced
garlic
½ onion (finely chopped) 6
tablespoons of butter
¼ cup (room temperature) sour
cream
1 cup of heavy whipping
cream
3 tablespoons of fresh
lemon juice
½ teaspoon of hot sauce
⅔ cups of freshly grated
pecorino cheese
⅔ cups of shredded
mozzarella cheese
½ cup shredded white
cheddar cheese
½ teaspoon of Tamika
Scott's "All-Purpose" Fuse
½ teaspoon of Tamika
Scott's "Vegetable" Fuse

Directions

1. Preheat oven to 350°F.
2. Make sure spinach liquid is drained.
3. In a large nonstick pan, melt butter over medium heat.
4. Add onion, cook until soft.
5. Add garlic and stir for 2 minutes.
6. Add flour and stir for 2 minutes.
7. Gradually whisk in heavy whipping cream and chicken broth, bring to a boil.
8. Add lemon juice, hot sauce, and Vegetable Fuse. Stir 1 minute.
9. Add Pecorino Romano cheese and mozzarella cheese. Stir until cheese has melted.
10. Stir in sour cream and fold in spinach, sprinkle All-Purpose Fuse on top.
11. Transfer mixture to a grease baking dish.
12. Sprinkle white cheddar cheese evenly on top.
13. Place in oven and bake 8-12 minutes.
14. Serve hot with tortilla chips, salsa, or sour cream.

Lobsters

My husband and I have committed to at least a once-a-month date night. A night where we are all alone. No Kids, No Pets, No Friends, No Phones, No Distractions! Just me and my husband. A date to us doesn't necessarily mean going out. We love staying in, connecting in a mental, physical, and spiritual way. Having each other's undivided attention allows us to reconnect over and over again. Every date night is different. We may put on our pajamas, pop popcorn, hold hands and reminisce about the day we met, how we fell in love, and who said I love you first.

On other dates, we go to our karaoke room and sing our little hearts out. We may even play a board game or a card game, or we may go to the kitchen and cook a fun meal together. Cooking is my love language, and food can be sexy. My husband always lets me pick what we're eating. This particular night I allowed him to choose, and to my surprise, he decided on my Freaky Fried Lobster Tails, my Lemon Garlic Seared Asparagus, and my Coconut Ginger Jazmine Rice. What a romantic night.

Sauteed Lemon Garlic Asparagus

Ingredients

1 lb. of asparagus
2 tablespoons cooking olive oil
2 teaspoons of minced garlic
2 tablespoon Tamika Scott's "Vegetable" Southern Fuse
½ Fresh lemon Juice
Shredded parmesan cheese (optional for garnishing)

Directions

1. In a large skillet, over medium heat, add oil. Then add asparagus to the pan.
2. Add minced garlic on top of asparagus. Season with Vegetable Fuse. Cover for 2 minutes.
3. Turn asparagus and season with Vegetable Fuse. Squeeze lemon juice on—cover for 2 minutes. Turn off heat.
4. Add parmesan cheese - optional

Ingredients

2 cups of jasmine Rice
2 cups of coconut milk
1 ½ cup of water
1 tablespoon of fresh ginger
1 tablespoon of minced garlic
1 teaspoon of sea salt
½ tablespoon of granulated sugar
1 teaspoon of onion powder
1 tablespoon of white pepper
¼ cup of grated sweetened coconut
2 tablespoons of butter

Directions

1. In a medium strainer, rinse the jasmine rice in cold water 3-4 times (to remove the starch). Allow drying.
2. In a large pot with a tight-fitting lid, bring coconut milk, water, sugar to a boil.
3. Add butter and allow it to melt.
4. Add ginger, garlic, sea salt, onion powder, and white pepper. Stir and bring to a boil.
5. Add rice and stir.
6. Immediately reduce heat to a simmer, cover tightly with a lid, and continue simmering for 15 minutes or until the liquid is absorbed.
7. Remove from heat and let stand about 4 minutes.
8. Fluff rice lightly with a fork and combine cooked rice with grated coconut.
9. Mix gently and serve warm.

Freaky Fried Lobster Tails

Ingredients

2 cups all-purpose flour
2 cups cornmeal
2 tablespoons Tamika Scott's "Seafood" Fuse
1 teaspoon Tamika Scott's "Cajun" Southern Fuse (garnish at the end)
4 -5 lobster tails cleaned and halved while leaving in shell
Vegetable Oil (for deep frying)

Directions

1. Thoroughly dry the lobster tails with paper towels.
2. In a large bowl, combine the flour, cornmeal, and seafood fuse. Blend well.
3. Place one lobster tail at a time in the bowl and coat exceptionally well.
4. Heat vegetable oil in a deep-fryer or large skillet to 365°F
5. Place one coated lobster tail at a time into the oil. Cook for 4 -6 minutes each; the coating should be lightly brown.
6. Remove the lobster tails from the grease and place them on paper towels. Sprinkle a dash of Tamika Scott's "Cajun" Southern Fuse on the tails to enhance the flavor and enjoy.

Drunk' N Grilled Oysters

Oysters

Oysters, oysters, oysters. I always say that with a smile. Vitamin D and Zinc in oysters help with arousal, libido, and one's sex drive. Vitamin C improves blood flow, and D-Aspartic Acid is essential for healthy testosterone levels and strong erections. With that being said, let's get right to my Grilled Oysters (with slices of buttered grilled French bread).

Drunk' N Grilled Oysters

Ingredients

12 fresh shucked oysters (scrubbed and cleaned)
1 stick of butter
½ of a fresh lemon juice
1 ½ teaspoon minced garlic
1 tablespoon of white cooking wine
½ teaspoon salt
½ teaspoon pepper
½ teaspoon Tamika Scott's Cajun Fuse
½ cup of parmesan cheese Hot sauce (of your choice)
1 loaf of French bread (sliced diagonally and buttered on both sides)

Directions

1. Preheat your grill to 400-450°F
2. In a medium saucepan, melt butter.
3. Add lemon juice, wine, garlic, salt, and pepper, and fuse. Stir well.
4. Take saucepan from heat.
5. Place oysters directly overheat (shell down).
6. With a big spoon, add the butter mixture (be careful, flames will rise. This is what you want it to do, as your mate!)
7. Add more butter sauce.
8. Add parmesan cheese.
9. Close grill for 3 minutes or until the cheese mixture begins to bubble.
10. Carefully remove oysters with heat-resistant grill gloves or tongues.
11. Place buttered bread on the grill for 1 to 2 minutes per side.
12. Remove bread from grill
13. Take oyster out of the shell and put it on top of grilled bread.
14. Dash of hot sauce on top, eat and enjoy.

Chocolate

Did you know that this delicious, rich, decadent treat grows on trees? Before it is fermented, sun-dried, roasted, pressed, and mixed with sugars and other ingredients, it is first a seed/bean from the fruit of a Cacao tree. The Cacao bean is the main ingredient in the process of making chocolate. Chocolate has its benefits. It has a positive effect on one's mood. It makes you feel good, and it provides energy. It is a libido booster and also contains antioxidants. The cocoa in chocolate increases blood flow through relaxed blood vessels and arteries, which send blood to all the right areas of the body. Try my Charming Chocolate Martini to get your blood flowing.

Mika's Charming Chocolate Martini

Mika's Charming Chocolate Martini

Ingredients

8 oz. martini glass
1 ½ oz. of vanilla vodka
1½ oz. of chocolate liqueur
21 oz. of crème de cocoa
½ oz. Hershey's chocolate syrup
2oz. of half and half
Shaker
Ice
Cocoa (for glass rim)
chocolate syrup (for glass rim)
white granulated sugar (for glass rim)
2 Small plates

Directions

1. Using one of the small plates, squeeze chocolate syrup in the corner of the plate. Carefully rim the top of the glass with the syrup.
2. On the other small plate, combine sugar and cocoa to make sweet. Make sure the sweet cocoa is spread out and is wider than the glass you are rimming.
3. Carefully dip the rim of the glass in the sweet cocoa. Then, twist, making sure to coat the entire edge of the glass.
4. Raise the glass from the plate and drizzle Hershey chocolate syrup vertically in martini from the middle to the bottom. Neatly
5. In a shaker, add ice and ingredients. Shake 35- 40 times fast.
6. Strain shaker in glass and enjoy!

Carrots

Everyone knows that carrots are suitable for eyesight. Did you know the antioxidants in carrots slow down the aging process? Carrots are also proven to keep the prostate gland healthy at the same time purifying the blood. One carrot a day keeps heart disease at bay. In the menIs department, carrots improve male fertility. They are known to treat

erectile dysfunction. Let's just say carrots should be a man's best friend.

Honey

Honey is an aphrodisiac! It helps produce testosterone in men and estrogen in women. It is a natural sweetener, giving it less of an impact on your blood sugar. Honey is rich in Vitamin B2 and Vitamin B1, which help fuel the body by converting carbs into sugar. Finally, it's said that honey keeps your skin radiant and you, young-looking. Now, let's celebrate the importance of honey and carrots with my Honey Glazed Carrots!

Honey Glazed Carrots

Ingredients

7-8 carrots (whole and thin) 2½ tablespoons of butter
2 tablespoons of honey
3½ tablespoons of brown sugar
Pinch of salt and pepper to taste

Directions

1. Rinse carrots in cold water with a vegetable brush or your fingers. Cut off the top and keep for garnishing—dry carrots off with a paper towel.
2. Melt butter in a large skillet over medium heat.
3. Add carrots.
4. Coat carrots in butter.
5. Add brown sugar and honey.
6. Turn carrots and mix until brown sugar dissolves.
7. Sprinkle in salt and pepper on both sides and glaze.
8. Cook carrots 10-15 minutes (glazing in between) or until your desired tenderness.
9. Serve immediately.

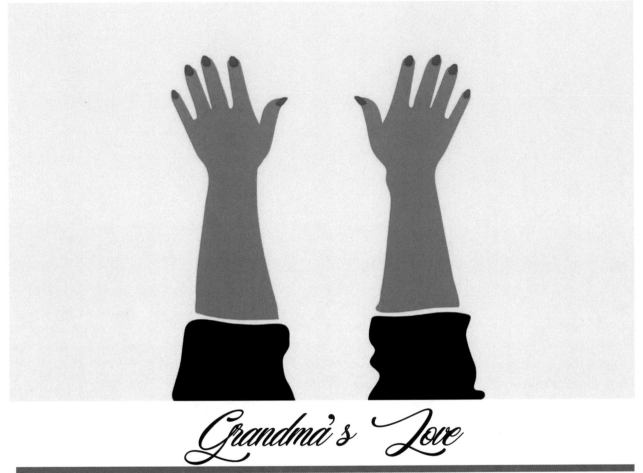

Grandma's Love

I remember driving from Atlanta to the country woods of Locust Grove, Georgia as a little girl. I would look out of the window with the biggest smile on my face because I knew we were on our way to my Grandparentsl home. I always knew when we were close because the air became crisp and clean. The air quality in the country was fresher to me than the air in the city. Grandma Mildred, the mother to all, was the designated cook and always welcomed everyone into their home. Visiting on weekends and Holidays was my favorite. Grandma Mildred is known to throw down in the kitchen. Baby! Some of the best homemade cooking you would ever taste. My grandfather, George Washington Ponder, (Why did his parents name him George Washington?)

Riding to the country to see my grandpa George and grandma Mildred was always a treat. My mom would pack a few sandwiches for us to eat just in case we got hungry along the way. The forty-five-minute drive seemed like an eternity when I was a kid. My father would sing silly songs, and my sister and I would sing along to make the long drive seem not so bad. I always knew when we were close and was eager to get out the car. Besides smelling the crisp, clean air the country constantly introduced, you could also see the cows a mile away and my grandma's garden. My grandmother would let me help her pull fresh vegetables out of the garden. One of my favorite vegetables to pick was corn on the cob.

Grandma Mildred taught me how to grab the ear, snap it against the stalk, then pull and twist it away from it to be released. Then, after picking just enough corn for the day, we would take them to the kitchen, rinse them in cold water and pull the silk from the ear. This was a long and tedious job, but I loved to help. It made me feel more mature, and I loved feeling like I was grown in a sense. By the time I was in high school, I was a pro (In my mind) when shucking corn. Now, I can do it with my eyes closed. I like to make mine sweet with a hint of pepper spice and a buttery flare. Everyone raves about my corn on the cob. And always get me to make it when we have gatherings and get-togethers.

Ingredients

(*Serving 6-8*)
6-8 ears of corn (husks and silks removed) whole or cut in half
2 cups of cold milk 1 cup of water
2 cups of sugar
1 tablespoon of Salt
1 tablespoon of black pepper
One stick of salted butter

Directions

1. Fill a large pot halfway with cold water, milk, sugar, salt, pepper, and butter. Stir.
2. Bring to a boil and stir.
3. Add corn and bring water back to a boil.
4. Cover for 8-10 minutes
5. Kernels should be crisp, tender, buttery, and sweet. Enjoy

New Orleans Baby

New Orleans is one of my top ten fun places to visit, especially during Mardi Gras. Attending the parades wearing a mask allowed me to be incognito and have as much fun as I wanted with my friends. My first Mardi Gras experience had me saying wow. I was shocked to see people walking in the street with their alcoholic beverages. Where I'm from, you can get arrested just by smelling like alcohol in the street. I've never seen so many breasts before in my life. Even with my mascaraed mask on, I didn't flash anyone for beads. It would've just been my luck to flash someone and my mask fell off. Nope, I didn't want that type of publicity.

So, I never had beads unless my good friend gave me a few of hers. Thank you boo, you know who you are. Besides their vibrant nightlife, New Orleans has the best Cajun-Creole food on the planet.

There were a few other times I've visited New Orleans, not for fun but business. My business trip to New Orleans in 2018 will always be an unforgettable one. X-scape had just gotten back together after an 18-year hiatus. We were invited to perform for the Essence Festival. I couldn't wait to finish the show so I could go over and eat a plate of delicious Jambalaya at my boo thang, Jayda's, house.

My group and I arrived in this little room known as the Super Lounge, which our manager was told the room held at least two thousand people. As our teams were getting us dressed, we heard a large crowd chanting, "We Want X-scape! We Want X-scape!" Smiling from ear to ear, the girls and I were flattered! Unaware of what was happening outside the dressing room, we went out on stage and gave a hell of a show! After our outstanding performance, we found out thousands of fans couldn't attend because the lounge had reached its capacity. And those fans who couldn't get in to see us we're livid. We were forced to stay in our dressing room until Essence security got everything under control.

That night we did a video apologizing to the fans that couldn't get in to see us. Even though it wasn't our fault that someone over the Essence Festival put us in that little room. They underestimated the love our fans had for us. I guess someone in control finally got the memo. They invited us back the following year to perform on the big stage. And we rocked the house again! Later that night, I enjoyed my friendls delicious Jambalaya. Now, I'm not from New Orleans, but I love making this dish. Sometimes I even wear my mask while eating eat to feel that New Orleans Vibe. Unfortunately, I can't make it as good as my boo, who's born and raised in "Norleans." I don't even make it as spicy as the natives, but this is my Cajun rendition of Jambalaya. Feel free to add or take away whatever you like.

.

Barbecue shrimp is another one of New Orleans's signature dishes. My first-time having this famous Louisiana specialty was at a gathering over my friend, Anthony Appleberry's, home. It was a potluck night where everyone brought over their favorite dish. As we called him, the Alps always bragged about his barbecue shrimp, so I couldn't wait to see if his bragging was in vain or not. I snuck into the kitchen, grabbed a fork to steal a piece of shrimp right out of the closed lid pot. Instead of finding barbecue shrimp, I found shrimp in what looked to be a buttery lemon sauce. "Where's the barbecue shrimp?" I yelled from the kitchen. The Alps and a few other New Orleans natives came into the kitchen and pointed at the pot. "Well, where's the barbecue sauce?" I asked. Seconds later, everyone burst out in laughter.

The Alps chuckled as he explained that Barbecue shrimp came from the spicy, smoky flavor when cooked in black pepper and Worcestershire sauce. I took my fork and continued to steal a shrimp. The shell on the shrimp almost made it hard to get with my knife. Before I could ask him why he left the body on the shrimp, he started giving me a lecture about the importance of keeping the shell on while cooking to retain its flavor. And how the shell protects the shrimp from overcooking. I can't remember anything after that because I was too busy peeling the shell away from the shrimp and plopping it into my mouth. It was buttery, with a hint of lemon, followed by a smoky barbecue spice taste. Ok, now it made sense, and it was delicious!

I underestimated the flavor of the "non-barbecued sauced" barbecue shrimp. I asked him repeatedly what spices he used, but he refused to tell me. So, I took my time and ate as many shrimps as I could that night until I figured it out. Then, of course, I added my little twist to it. So now my barbecue shrimp will give him a run for his money!

Ingredients

2 pounds of large shrimp, raw, peeled, and deveined

4 cups of butter

⅓ cup of olive oil

2 tablespoons of Worcestershire sauce

2 tablespoons of fresh-squeezed lemon juice

2 tablespoons of minced garlic

1 tablespoon of Tamika Scott "Barbecue" Southern Fuse

1 tablespoon of Tamika Scott's "Cajun" Southern Fuse

2 tablespoons of black pepper

½ teaspoon of (your favorite) hot sauce

1 small onion long sliced

1 lemon cut 4 ways

1 teaspoon of pink Himalayan salt

½ cup of dry white wine

2 drops of liquid smoke

4 sprigs of fresh rosemary

1 Loaf of French bread sliced (for dipping)

Garlic butter (for French bread).

Directions

1. Preheat oven to 350
2. In a large skillet (make sure you have the lid for later) on medium-high, melt butter. Add olive oil, onion, and minced garlic. Sauté for 1 minute. Stirring constantly.
3. Add Worcestershire sauce, lemon juice, Cajun Southern Fuse, black pepper, pink salt, hot sauce, and wine. Bring to a boil.
4. While waiting for the sauce to boil. Slice French Bread. Spread garlic butter on both sides. Place in preheated oven for 3-4 minutes or until lightly brown. Make sure to watch it. Turn and bake 3-4 more minutes or until desired toasted color. Take out of the oven and set aside.
5. As the pot begins to boil, add lemon slices and liquid smoke— Cook for 1 minute.
6. Add shrimp, continuously stirring for 3 minutes, add Barbecue Fuse. Cover for three more minutes or until shrimp is opaque.
7. Uncover and add rosemary sprigs and remove from heat. Serve immediately
8. Dip French bread in buttery barbecue juice for a treat.

My Sayda Baby Jambalaya

Ingredients

(1) 14 oz.
andouille smoked
sausage, sliced
1 pound of large
shrimp, raw,
peeled, and
deveined
14.5 oz. petite
diced can of
tomatoes
3 cups of rice
Half of a yellow
onion, chopped
2 tablespoons of olive
oil
6½ cups of
chicken broth
1 green bell pepper,
seeded and chopped
1 celery stalk,
chopped
½ teaspoon of
minced garlic
3 tablespoons of
Tamika Scott's
"Cajun" Southern
Fuse
1 teaspoon of salt
1 teaspoon of
black pepper
Optional- your
favorite hot sauce

Directions

1. In a large dutch pan, heat olive oil on medium to high heat.
2. Add onions, celery, and bell peppers. Sauté 2 minutes.
3. Add garlic. Cook for 1 minute.
4. Add sausages. Cook for 1 minute.
5. Add 2 tablespoons of Cajun Southern Fuse, black pepper, and salt.
6. Stir in chicken broth, diced tomatoes, and rice.
7. Add 1 tablespoon of Cajun Southern Fuse.
8. Cover and cook for 15 minutes. Uncover and stir.
9. Add shrimp. (Optional add hot sauce) and cover for 8 minutes or until shrimp is opaque and rice is tender.
10. Taste and adjust seasonings. Add a touch more of Cajun Southern Fuse if desired.
11. Serve and enjoy.

Jambalaya Egg Rolls

I always have leftovers after making my Jayda Baby Jambalaya. So, I like to make Jambalaya Egg Rolls. I add a few key ingredients to make this an even more delicious dish. It's also one of my family's favorites.

Jambalaya Egg Rolls

Ingredients

2 cups of leftover Jambalaya

10 egg roll wrappers (or more until all filling is gone)

2 cups of shredded cheese (optional)

2 cups of small shrimp, cleaned, deveined, cooked

1½ cups of crab meat (imitation crab is finely cut)

5 cups of canola oil (or enough to cover about 2 inches in the pan)

1 cup of water (will help seal egg roll wrapper)

¼ measuring cup (optional)

Sweet chili sauce (for dipping)

Directions

1. Preheat canola oil to 370°F
2. Lay 1 egg roll wrapper on a plate
3. Fill your ¼ cup measuring cup with cheese, shrimp, jambalaya, and crab meat. (If you're not using a measuring cup, make sure you use a small amount enough to roll without filling falling out). Add to center of egg roll.
4. Dip your clean fingertip in the water, dab a little bit on all of the corners of the egg roll. This will help bind it together. Next, fold the left bottom corner up to the middle of the wrapper. Then fold the right corner towards the center as well. Finally, press and tightly roll upwards to close the egg roll.
5. Repeat with remaining egg roll wraps and filling.
6. Fry egg rolls 1-2minutes, turn and cook 1-2 more minutes or until golden brown.
7. Drain on a paper towel.

If you're using an air fryer:

1. Spray your air fryer basket with olive oil cooking spray.
2. Place your egg rolls in the basket and lightly spray the top of your egg rolls.
3. Cook at 400°F for 6 minutes, then turn your egg roll. Then cook for an additional 6 minutes.

To Ve or not to Vegan

My superstar daughter, rapper, and actress, Young Niyah, gradually removed meat from her diet. She no longer eats beef, pork, lamb, and a few dairy products. I look at her stages of eating, almost like a butterfly. She already experienced the egg stage, which occurred first. At an earlier age, Niyah could eat anything without consequences. Before now, she didn't have to worry about gaining weight or counting calories. That stage is long gone. The pescatarian, caterpillar stage is where she's presently in; soon, she will be in the cocoon stage, but until then, I have more than enough time to perfect my vegan dishes, and she's the right person to test them out, being she has eaten meat and she will compare every vegan dish to the non-vegan. Therefore, they have to taste similar or better! With Niyah being my taste tester, I have to perfect these recipes because baby girl will let me know if it's good or not! By the time she's a full beautiful butterfly, vegan, I will be the master chef of vegan cuisines!

Ingredients

*1 bag of frozen
cauliflower rice
1 small onion chopped
1 cup frozen peas & carrots
(thawed)
¼ cup frozen broccoli florets
(thawed)
3 tablespoon soy sauce
⅛ teaspoon Tamika Scott's
"Vegetable" Southern Fuse
2 small eggs (optional) Olive
or Canola oil
One packet of Fried Rice
Seasoning*

Directions

1. Heat 2 teaspoons of oil in a large nonstick skillet over medium heat. Add the eggs and a pinch of Tamika Scott's "Vegetable" Southern Fuse and scramble until the eggs are fully cooked. Transfer to a small plate and set aside. Wipe the pan clean.

2. Add 3 tablespoons of oil to the pan and set over medium heat. Add the onions until softened but not browned, 3-4 minutes.

3. Add the cauliflower, soy sauce, and all-purpose fuse. Cook, often stirring, for about 3 minutes. Add the peas, carrots, broccoli, and fried rice seasoning. Continue cooking until the cauliflower "rice" is tender-crisp and the vegetables are warmed through, a few minutes. Stir in the eggs. Serve hot.

Niyah's Fried Orange Sauce'd Tofu

Ingredients

*2 firm Tofu (for my meat-
eating kids, I substitute tofu
with*
*2lbs of boneless chicken
thighs and follow the same
recipe)*
Tofu Breading
1 tablespoon salt
1 tablespoon white pepper
*1 cup cornstarch (breading
mixture)*
3 cups of flour
1 large egg
*1½ cups of water (for
breading mixture)*
*2 tablespoons of oil (for
breading mixture)*
Orange Sauce
*1 teaspoon vegetable oil (for
Orange Sauce)*
*¼ teaspoon chili flakes
(optional)*
½ teaspoon fresh ginger
*1 tablespoon fresh minced
garlic*
¼ cup granulated sugar
¼ cup brown sugar
¼ cup orange juice
¼ cup white vinegar
2 tablespoons soy sauce
2 tablespoons water
2 tablespoons cornstarch
*1 teaspoon vegetable oil (for
orange sauce)*
1 teaspoon sesame oil

Directions

1. Drain tofu and pat dry. Cut tofu into 1-inch cubes.
2. In a medium bowl, mix cornstarch, salt, white pepper and flour
3. One at a time, mix in the egg and 1½ cups of water and 2 tablespoons of oil.
4. Add tofu to the mixture. Put in refrigerator for thirty minutes.
5. Heat oil to 350°F; when oil is hot, fry tofu in small batches, a few pieces at a time.
6. Drain tofu on a paper towel. Set aside.
7. Prepare the orange sauce. In a medium skillet or wok, over medium heat, add 1 teaspoon of vegetable oil. Stir in chili flakes, ginger, garlic, granulated sugar, brown sugar, orange juice, vinegar, and soy sauce.
8. In a small cup or bowl, mix 2 tablespoons of water and 2 tablespoons of cornstarch. Add mixture to skillet and stir. Add one teaspoon of sesame oil to sauce and stir.
9. Lightly toss the tofu in orange sauce. Make sure to get delicious sauce on the entire tofu. Serve immediately and enjoy— This pairs well with Niyah's Cauliflower Fried Rice.

Mermaids Only No "Fish" Allowed Sandwich

Ingredients

2 slices of gluten-free oat bread

1 can of chickpeas (drained and rinsed)

1 dill pickle (finely chopped)
1 tablespoon of Dijon mustard

2½ tablespoons of vegan mayo

¼ cup of red onions (finely chopped)

1 tablespoon of Tamika Scott's "Seafood" Southern Fuse

1 tablespoon of lemon juice Sprinkle of sea salt

Sprinkle of black pepper (For sandwich)

2 slices of gluten-free oat bread

Lettuce

Tomato slices

Pickle (dill or sweet, your preference)

Directions

1. Place drained chickpeas in a medium mixing bowl. Roughly mash with a fork.
2. Add mustard, mayo, pickles, onions, Seafood Fuse, lemon juice, sea salt, and black pepper. Mix.
3. Taste to approve seasoning. If needed, add more mayo for extra creaminess.
4. Lightly toast sandwich bread. Add mermaid mix to bread and top it with lettuce, tomato, pickle, and enjoy!

Ingredients

1 (12 oz.) box of tri-color Rotini pasta

1 cup cucumber (cut in cubes)

1 (8oz) crab meat fresh or imitation

1 cup of crumbled feta cheese

2 tablespoons of Tamika Scott's "All-Purpose" Southern Fuse

1 cup of Italian salad dressing (feel free to use more or less)

1 cup of grape tomatoes

1 cup of black olives (sliced in half)

1 tablespoon vegetable oil

Directions

1. Fill a large pot halfway with water. Bring water to a boil. Add "All-Purpose" Fuse and vegetable oil. Allow boiling for a few minutes.
2. Add rotini pasta to boiling water. Cook al dente, 8-10 minutes.
3. Drain pasta, allow cooling.
4. While pasta is cooling, cut black olives in half, and cucumber in cubes.
5. After pasta cools, combine pasta, olives, cucumber, grape tomatoes, feta cheese, and crab meat in a large bowl.
6. Pour in Italian dressing and stir to coat the entire pasta.
7. Serve and enjoy or put in the refrigerator for a few hours in a covered container.

Grandma Alma's Visit

4 feet 11 inches stood my grandma, Alma Kate. She was my father's mom, whom I truly adored! She was short but had a big personality. Her laugh was always heard over a crowd. One of my fondest memories of my grandmother was when she spent the night with me after church service one Friday night. My grandmother broke her hip and had to move in with my father, Pastor Randolph Scott.

My father was going out of town for a church conference over the weekend, so my grandmother came to stay with me until he returned that following Monday. Grandma Alma Kate loved her beer but couldn't have any because my father wasn't purchasing any alcohol being a minister. I wanted to make her stay memorable, so I went to the store and bought her three 24 oz—cans of her favorite beer, Old English 800. I also purchased her favorite fish, cod; sides, green beans, and my southern version of Mexican rice.

I knew she had not had a drink since she moved in with my father over a year ago. I was going to make sure her stay was one to remember. The morning before she came to my house, I put her beers in the refrigerator to be ice cold. After my dad dropped Grandma Alma Kate off, he told me she hadn't eaten much that day. I told him I would make sure she ate. I hurried him off to his car. As soon as he pulled off, I rushed back into the house, turned the tv on to Grandma Alma Kates's favorite show, Sandford and Son.

Then I went into the fridge to retrieve one of her cold beers. As soon as she saw the can, she flashed the biggest smile ever. "MIKA!" She whispered, looking up at me. She grabbed the can and closed her eyes. She kissed the can and slowly opened it. As soon as it opened, you could hear the pssssssssshhhh sound. Grandma stared at that can as if a tall, handsome man was standing in front of her. She took a big gulp. "Ahhh, this is good Mika. Thank You!" I told her she was welcome and that this was our little secret. I went into the kitchen to begin cooking. Fifteen minutes later, I went to check on my grandmother, and she was laughing her little heart out. She handed me an empty can and asked if I had any more beer. Before answering, I slipped back into the kitchen and retrieved her second can of beer. Once again, she kissed the can. I laughed and walked back into the kitchen. Minutes later, I prepared my salsa rice and green beans and began prepping the fish to be sautéed. I smiled to myself, hearing my grandmother laugh even harder.

I was so glad she was enjoying herself. I became alarmed when her laughs turned into a constant cough. I went back into the living room only to see my grandmother leaned over laughing at a commercial. I looked and didn't find anything funny. Oh, No! My grandmother was drunk. How?!? Off of two beers? I panicked, knowing my father could call and check on her any minute now.

I ran into the kitchen to finish cooking. I needed to feed her to soak up the alcohol that was swimming in her tummy. Soon as I finished cooking, I made her plate. Surprisingly she ate all of her food. Shortly after, she took her bath and fell asleep before my dad could call. Whew, that was a close one!

Ingredients

1 cup of long grain rice (uncooked)
2 cups of chicken broth
3 tablespoon of butter
½ cup of salsa (Pace Picante salsa)
1 teaspoon of minced garlic
½ teaspoon of Tamika Scott's "All-Purpose" Southern Fuse

Directions

1. Over medium-high heat, in a large pot, combine all ingredients and stir.
2. Bring to a boil, then cover. Reduce heat to low. Allow simmering for 25 minutes. Do Not lift the lid off the pot.
3. Remove from heat; keep the top on rice for 10 minutes—no peeking whatsoever.
4. After 10 minutes, remove the lid from the pot and fluff out the rice with a fork.

Mika's Cajun Codfish

Ingredients

8 cod fillets
1 lemon
1 onion
2 green bell
peppers
2 red bell pepper
Tamika Scott's "Seafood"
Southern Fuse (season
Fish) Tamika Scott's
"Cajun" Southern Fuse
(season vegetables)
1 tablespoon of olive oil

Directions

1. Squeeze lemon juice on cod. Season both sides of the fillets with Seafood Fuse. Set aside.
2. Slice onions and bell peppers into long strips.
3. In a large frying pan on medium-high heat, add olive oil and half of your onions and bell peppers.
4. Season with Cajun Fuse. Place cod fillets on top of the bed of vegetables. Then lay the rest of the vegetables on top of the cod and Season with Cajun Fuse.
5. Cover and let simmer for 25 minutes. Carefully, with a spatula, flip cod over on top of the vegetable. Squeeze lemon juice onto cod and season with Cajun Fuse. Cover pan and cook for 12 minutes or until fish is fully cooked through.

Mika's Southern Green Beans

Ingredients

1½ lbs. of green beans
1 smoked turkey leg
1 yellow onion (sliced)
2 cups of chicken broth
2 cups of water
1 teaspoons of minced garlic
1 tablespoon of Tamika Scott's "Vegetable" Southern Fuse
¼ teaspoon of Salt (optional)
¼ teaspoon of pepper

Directions

1. In a large pot over medium-high heat, bring chicken broth, water, smoked turkey leg, salt, and pepper to a boil—Cook for 20 minutes.
2. Add onions and Vegetable Fuse. Stir. Bring to a boil.
3. Add green beans and minced garlic. Stir and bring to a boil.
4. Turn heat down to medium—cover and cook for 35 minutes.

Trip to Jamaica

My first visit to Jamaica was with my husband, Darnell, who was only my boyfriend at the time. When I tell you, he spared no expense, none! First-class seats on Delta Airlines, limousine ride from the airport with some of my favorite snacks inside. All of my favorite songs played as we drove to the beautiful, gated all-inclusive resort. Live music greeted us as we got out of the limousine. A well-dressed young man was standing outside and handed my husband our key to our suite.

A beautiful young Jamaican girl handed me a chilled glass of pina colada, garnished with a pineapple on the side of the glass. "Welcome, Darnell and Tamika," she said in her cute Jamaican accent. I was blown away by how exotic the resort was. The bellman took our bags out of the trunk, and we were escorted inside, down a long hallway, into a dining area to a table decorated with beautiful flowers. I sat, and the waitress placed my napkin in my lap. The smell of curry chicken danced from the kitchen as another waiter brought out my plate. I couldn't wait to eat my curry chicken deliciously laying over a bed of rice, two sweet plantains, and a side of vegetables.

Darnell's dish was beautifully plated with Jerk Chicken, rice, and peas with a side of vegetables. Everything was so perfect that I pinched myself. Darnell laughed at me because I pinched myself a little too hard. I wanted to make sure this was real. I took a deep breath, trying to keep my composure. We had only been dating for a year, and I didn't want him to see me emotional. He grabbed my hand and said a lovely prayer. Yes, I love a man that prays and acknowledges My God. Had he asked me to marry him at that moment, I might have said yes. I knew I needed to eat, and in a hurry, because I felt whatever it was in that pina colada.

Like Beyoncel s song, "I've been drinking, I've been drinking. I get filthy when that liquor gets into me," and I needed to eat! My curry chicken plate was picture-perfect. It looked as if it should've been in a cookbook. I pulled the water closed to me, just in case my curry was too spicey. I watched Darnell take a bite and close his eyes as he was chewing. Either he was tired from our long flight, or he was enjoying his jerk chicken. I took a bite, and to my surprise, it wasn't as spicy as I thought. It was delicious. After eating all of my food and half of his, the chef came out of the kitchen and introduced the dessert brought out to us. I quickly asked him how he prepared the curry so well and creamy. To my surprise, he told me step by step.

It was way too many steps for me. I loved the dish, but I refused to work on one dish for more than an hour. When I got home, I knew I wanted to find a way to prepare a dish as good as the natives of Jamaica, and I also wanted to cut the steps in half without compromising the taste. So, here's my shortcut, Jaml n Curry Chicken. Along with a few other delicious entrées I had throughout the week of our vacation.

Ingredients

2 ¼ lbs. of chicken (boneless thighs)

2 tablespoons Blue Mountain Curry Powder (to season chicken)

3 tablespoons Blue Mountain Curry Powder (for dutch oven)

2 tablespoons of Tamika Scott's "All-Purpose" Southern Fuse

4 tablespoons of Tamika Scott's "Poultry" Southern Fuse

3 tablespoons of cooking oil

2 cups of coconut milk

1 large yellow onion (chopped)

1 tablespoon of hot sauce

1 tablespoon of minced garlic

2 potatoes (cut in eight pieces)

Vinegar and water (to clean)

Directions

1. Cut chicken thighs into 4 pieces, wash with vinegar and water.
2. Combine chicken with 2 tablespoons of curry powder and Poultry Fuse. Set aside.
3. In a large cast-iron pot, add cooking oil. Turn heat on medium-high.
4. Once hot, add onions and occasionally stir for 2 minutes.
5. Now, add 3 tablespoons of curry powder and 2 tablespoons of the all-purpose fuse. Stir occasionally for 1 minute.
6. Add garlic and stir for 1 minute.
7. Add chicken and hot sauce. Sauté for 5 minutes.
8. Add the potatoes, often stirring for 3 minutes.
9. Add coconut milk and stir. Reduce heat to medium and cover for 20 minutes or until chicken is completely done.
10. Uncover and stir.

Ingredients

8 chicken legs or 3 pounds cut-up chicken
1 tablespoon of Tamika Scott's "Cajun" Southern Fuse
2 tablespoon Tamika Scott's "Barbeque" Southern Fuse
1 or more scotch bonnet pepper habaneros
6 cloves chopped garlic
1 medium onion coarsely chopped
3 medium chopped scallions
1 sprig of fresh thyme 1 scotch bonnet pepper (Optional)
1 tablespoon Soy Sauce
½ cup pineapple juice or water
2 tablespoons olive or canola oil

Directions

1. Clean and trim off excess fat from chicken, then season with Cajun Fuse, set the chicken aside.
2. Heat oil in a skillet over medium heat. Then add scotch bonnet pepper, and garlic. Sauté until it turns brown, about 2-3 minutes.
3. Add Barbeque Fuse and continue stirring until seasoning starts to combine thoroughly.
4. Place the mixture in a food processor or blender, add thyme, scallions, soy sauce, onion, and pineapple juice. Pulse for about 30 - 40 seconds until blended.
5. Combine the chicken and wet blend into a zip lock bag and refrigerate for at least 2 hours, preferably overnight.
6. When ready to bake, preheat the oven to 425°F. Remove chicken from the jerk marinade using tongs; save excess marinade. Arrange chicken legs out in a single layer in a pan lined with foil.
7. Bake chicken legs until cooked through and skin is crispy, about 45 minutes, turning the chicken at least once.
8. In a small saucepan, simmer (or microwave) the remaining jerk marinade for about 7 minutes, pour over chicken, cook an additional 15 minutes. Serve and enjoy.

Ingredients

2-3 lbs. oxtails (trimmed/washed)

2 tablespoons Tamika Scott's "Beef" Southern Fuse

4 tablespoons Blue Mountain Curry Powder

3 potatoes (cut in chunks) 3 carrots (chopped)

2 cups coconut milk 1 cup beef broth

4 cloves crushed garlic

½ cup medium sliced onion

5 sprigs thyme

4 bay leaf

1 Scotch Bonnet (optional)

Directions

1. Place oxtails, potatoes, carrots, onions, and garlic in your slow cooker.
2. Pour coconut milk and beef broth on top. Mix in Beef Fuse, curry powder, bay leaves, thyme sprigs, and scotch bonnet (if desired).
3. Cover and cook on high for 5 to 6 hours, stirring occasionally.
4. Taste and add more curry powder if desired. Serve warm over rice and enjoy!

Mika's Drinks

I'm known to throw parties of a lifetime! But the most exciting thing about coming to my celebrations is that my guest don't have to find a babysitter. Every party or gathering my husband and I have is family friendly. We always incorporate fun and entertainment for the younger kids, teenagers, and my adult friends and family. My favorite bartender and family friend, Tony Williams, tends every party we have. He is INCREDIBLE. After ordering one cocktail, he remembers exactly what every person asked for. Tony never lets a cup stay empty, and he always aims to please.

One funny story that stands out in my mind about Tony is the night of my 2019 New Year's Eve party. My husband gives me a two-drink maximum because he says I'm either sleepy or become too honest by my third drink.

Therefore, Tony makes my drinks with more juice and less alcohol. This particular evening, I complained to Tony about how weak my drink was. If I had a two-drink maximum, at least they should've been strong enough for me to get a buzz. A few minutes after complaining, I went Live on my Instagram page to wish my followers a Happy New Year and encourage them to continue to be great and trust in God for a blessed 2019. In the midst of my encouraging and ministering, Tony walks up to me and hands me a martini while saying, "See if this one's strong enough for you." I was speechless. With my mouth wide open, I didn't say anything for 4 or 5 seconds. Then, all of a sudden, everyone started going in on me in the comments section. Someone wrote, "Is That Jesus juice?" Another person typed, "What's in your cup Tamika?"

I went on to say that Jesus! first miracle was turning water into wine. And for people not to judge me because I'm a work in progress. Hahaha, then I added that the bible says wine is good for the heart. That's when another person wrote, "But You're Drinking a Martini!" After a few more minutes, I ended my Live, wishing everyone a Happy New Year. Bahahaha, I Love me some Tony and his mixology. So here are a few of me and hubby's favorite go-to adult beverages!

Ingredients

4 oz. champagne
2 oz. Cranberry Juice

Directions

1. Tilt champagne flute and pour champagne in glass.
2. Add Cranberry Juice and enjoy

Ingredients

8 cups of water
6 large lemons
1 ¾ cups sugar

Directions

1. Add 1 ½ cup lemon juice from fresh lemons to water and sugar in a pot and bring to a boil, reduce heat, and allow the mix to simmer for 5 -6 minutes.
2. Remove from heat, allow to cool, refrigerate overnight.

Blackberry Fetish Lemonade

Ingredients

10 oz. lemonade
2 oz. Pimm's Blackberry
&
Elderflower

Directions

1. Pour ingredients over ice, stir.
2. Garnish with blackberries (optional).

Ingredients

*1 scoop orange
sherbet
2 oz. pineapple juice
Champagne or Your
Favorite Sparkling Blend*

Directions

1. Blend sherbet and juice in a blender, pour in a champagne glass (leave room for champagne, more or less to your liking).
2. Top with Champagne & Enjoy!

Ingredients

2½ oz. Rum
3oz. Coco Lopez Cream
of Coconut
3 oz. pineapple
juice
1 cup of ice

Directions

1. Blend ingredients together in a blender, pour in a fancy glass, and garnish with a slice of pineapple.
2. This recipe can be made ahead of time and kept in the freezer. Remove 10 - 15 minutes from the freezer before serving.

Ingredients

*2 oz. Captain
Morgan
Orange/Vanilla Twist
2 scoops of vanilla ice
cream
2 scoops orange sherbet
2 oz. milk
Ice (if needed)*

Directions

1. Blend ingredients in a blender. Add ice if necessary to thicken.

2. This recipe can be made ahead of time and placed in the freezer. Remove from the freezer 10 - 15 minutes before serving.

3. This recipe can also be substituted with non-dairy ice cream and non-dairy milk.

Ingredients

2 oz. Vanilla Vodka
1 ½ oz. Fresh Lime Juice
4 tablespoons Coco
Lopez Cream of Coconut
2 oz. Pineapple Juice
2 scoops of Vanilla
Ice Cream
Ice (if needed)
3- 4 graham crackers

Directions

1. Crush graham crackers, except a half piece, set aside. Blend all other ingredients, add ice if needed to thicken.
2. After the mix is blended, fold in the graham cracker crumbs. Garnish with sliced lime and a half graham cracker.

Ingredients

2 oz. Vanilla Vodka
2.5 oz. Peach
Schnapps
1 oz. Amaretto
4 - 5 cubes of ice
2-3 graham
crackers (Garnish)
2 tablespoons Tamika
Scott's
"Sweetener" Southern Fuse
(Garnish)
Caramel sauce (Garnish)

Directions

1. Crush graham crackers into fine crumbs, mix with Sweetener Fuse, set aside.
2. Put liquid ingredients in a martini shaker with ice, shake vigorously.
3. Coat martini glass rim with caramel sauce, then dip the rim in graham cracker blend.
4. Strain shaker ingredients into the martini glass. Serve immediately.

Ingredients

1 ½ vanilla Vodka
4 oz. Creme de
Banana
1 oz. Irish Cream
½ Godiva Chocolate
Liquor
2 - 3 scoops of vanilla ice
cream
1 cup of Ice

Directions

1. Blend all ingredients in a blender.
2. Pour in a serving glass. Garnish with fresh banana slices.

Ingredients

2 oz. Limoncello Original
2 fresh
strawberries (muddled)
5 basil leaves
5 oz. Lemonade* (see
lemonade recipe below if you
want to make your own.
Ice

Directions

1. Place five basil leaves in lemonade and store them in the refrigerator overnight.
2. Muddle two fresh strawberries with a wooden spoon and place in a 9 oz. glass.
3. Pour limoncello and lemonade over strawberries, stir to mix well.
4. Add ice.
5. Garnish with a fresh strawberry and basil leaf.

Ingredients

2 oz. Vanilla Vodka
2.5 oz. Kahlua liqueur
1.5 oz. Godiva
chocolate liqueur
1 oz. Irish cream
2 scoops of vanilla
ice cream
Cocoa powder
(Garnish) Thick
chocolate sauce
(Garnish)

Directions

1. Blend all ingredients. Add one cup of ice if the blend needs thickening.
2. Coat glass rim with chocolate sauce, then dip the rim in cocoa powder.
3. Pour blended ingredients into a glass. Serve immediately.

Tamika's Apple Pie Sangria

Ingredients

1 green apple (cored and cubed)
1 red apple (cored and cubed)
1 sliced orange
1 (750 ml) bottle of Pinot Grigio
1 cup caramel Vodka
3 cups apple juice or apple cider
*¼ cup apple pie simple syrup**

Directions

1. Add all ingredients together in a large pitcher, refrigerate for at least 6 hours or overnight.

Ingredients

1 cup water
1 cup sugar
½ teaspoon cinnamon
¼ teaspoon nutmeg
¼ teaspoon cardamom
⅛ teaspoon allspice

Directions

1. Combine all ingredients in a medium saucepan, bring items to a boil, reduce heat then simmer.
2. For 10 minutes or until sugar is dissolved and a thicker syrup forms.

Ingredients

1 ½ oz. Tequila
¾ oz. Patron Citrónge
or Triple Sec
2 oz. red wine
2 oz. Olive Garden
Berry Sangria Mix
4 oz. Sour Mix
Ice

Directions

1. Mix all ingredients in a shaker. Pour over ice. Enjoy.

Ingredients

1 ½ oz. Tequila
¾ oz. Patron Citrónge
or Triple Sec
2 jalapeno rings (seeds removed)
3 cucumber slices
4 oz. sour mix
Sugar (Garnish optional) Ice

Directions

1. Muddle jalapeno rings and cucumber slices together with a wooden spoon or cocktail muddler.
2. Place in a shaker.
3. Add all ingredients to the shaker, shake vigorously. Add sugar to the rim of the margarita glass, pour in ingredients from the shaker into the margarita glass.
4. Garnish with cucumber.

Ingredients

2 oz. watermelon vodka
4 oz. sour Mix
2 slices of watermelon
2-3 cubes of ice

Directions

1. Muddle watermelon with a wooden spoon.
2. Combine all ingredients in a shaker, shake vigorously.
3. Pour contents from shaken in a tall glass with ice.

Ingredients

*4 oz. watermelon
vodka*
4 oz. sour mix
*4 slices of
watermelon*
1 cup of ice

Directions

1. Blend all ingredients in a blender until slushy, serve in your favorite glass, and enjoy.

Ingredients

2 oz. peach vodka
6oz. sweet tea
Ice

Directions

1. In a tall glass, add ice.
2. Pour peach vodka over ice, then add sweet tea.
3. Garnish with sliced fresh peaches.

Ingredients

5 oz. champagne (or your favorite sparkling beverage)

3 fresh peeled peach wedges (if not in season, use

2 oz. peach nectar)

Directions

1. Muddle peaches with a wooden spoon or cocktail muddler.
2. Place muddled peaches in the bottom of a champagne glass, top with champagne (or sparkling beverage).
3. Happy New Year

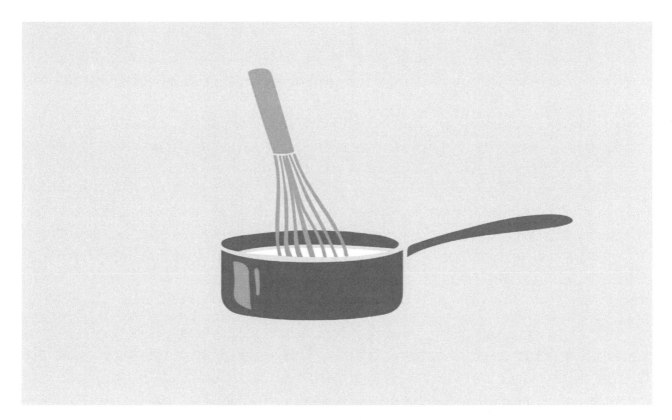

Treats Treats Treats

My Aunt Neat is the oldest and shortest out of ten kids by my grandmother, Mildred. When Aunt Neat looks at you, you would swear she could read your mind and see through your soul! When I was younger, I thought she was the meanest aunt out of all my aunties. Every time my mom dropped me and my sister off at her house, I would feel like I was having an anxiety attack. I would go inside and sit on the couch and would be scared to go to the restroom. Finally, one particular day she told us we could go outside in the backyard to play. My sister got up and went to the back. I sat still on the couch, hesitant to move. My aunt came into the living room where I was and looked at me with her beady eyes. "You're not going outside?" "No, ma'am," I said, trembling. "Well, come here!" She said, as her voice echoed in my heart.

She was walking towards the kitchen. I was sweating, hoping I wasn't about to get in trouble for not going outside when she told me to. As I turned the corner, Aunt Neat stood in front of the refrigerator with a big wooden spoon. I immediately panicked when I saw her, thinking she was going to hit me with it. Anyone from the south knows that if you disobeyed your parents or a family member, there would be consequences. You would get a whooping, or something is thrown at you. I had been whipped with a belt, a switch, a fly swat, and a shoe. Thinking this wooden spoon wouldn't be much pain. I closed my eyes, not to see when she was going to strike. But I was startled by what came next. "Open your eyes and open your mouth. I Want you to taste this."

I opened my eyes, and to my surprise, it was a spoon full of banana pudding staring back at me. This wasn't any ordinary pudding. It was fluffy and sweet. I've never had banana pudding as good as this before. "You like it?" She asked. "Oh yes, ma'am!" I said with my eyes closed. That was the best banana pudding ever! After that moment, I took a real good look at my Aunt Neat. She smiled at me, and that's when I realized she wasn't mean after all. When she talks to you, she looks you right in your eyes. I was always intimidated by that, but that's just her way of communicating. I thought my Aunt Neat was mean all these years, only to find out she was sweet. And because of her, I know how to make my Sweet Neat- No Bake- Banana pudding!

Ingredients

1 box (5.1 oz.) instant banana cream pudding mix 3 packages Pepperidge Farm Chessman Cookies or vanilla wafers
7 medium bananas sliced
1 can (14) oz. sweetened condensed milk
3 cups of heavy whipping cream
2 cups of milk
1 teaspoon Pure Vanilla Extract
1 tablespoon sugar

Directions

1. In a large bowl, whisk milk, pudding, and sweet condense milk, until smooth. Set aside for 5 minutes
2. In a medium bowl, add heavy whipping cream, sugar and pure vanilla extract. Beat with mixer, on medium until soft and fluffy.
3. Fold whipping cream into the pudding mixture.
4. Line the bottom of a 9X13 pan with Pepperidge Farm cookies.
5. Top with bananas.
6. Spread half of the pudding mixture over top of bananas.
7. Repeat layering, add cookies, bananas, and pudding.
8. Add cookies on top
9. Cover and refrigerate for 3 hours or until chilled.

Ingredients

½ cup of salted butter (melted)
½ cup granulated sugar
¼ cup brown sugar
2 teaspoons vanilla extract
1 large egg
1 ¾ cup all-purpose flour
½ teaspoon baking powder
1 cup semi-sweet chocolate chips
Cookie scoop
Silicone spatula

Directions

1. Preheat oven to 350°F
2. Mix (melted, not hot) butter with the sugar until well combined in a large bowl.
3. Add Vanilla and egg, then stir.
4. Add flour and baking soda. Mix until the dough is soft and a little sticky.
5. Stir in chocolate chips. Scrape sides of the bowl with a spatula and continue to mix.
6. Scoop out dough and place 2 inches apart on the cookie sheet.
7. Bake 10-12 minutes, or until cookies are golden brown. We like to take them out of the oven when puffy and look a little under-baked in the middle.

Ingredients

Pizie Crust (when I don't have much time, I also use a 9 inch, original-not deep dish, frozen pie crust from grocery store)
1 cup all-purpose flour (and a little more for dusting)
⅛ teaspoon salt (optional)
⅓ cup (5 tablespoons and 1 teaspoon) of cold unsalted butter (ICE COLD) cut into cubes
¼ teaspoon Tamika Scott's "Sweetener" Southern Fuse
½ teaspoon granulated sugar
4 tablespoons water (cold)
1 sheet parchment paper
1 pie crust rolling mat
1 rolling pin
(Optional) Strawberries and whip cream for garnishing
Pizie Filling
4 medium sweet potatoes (cooked, skin removed, mashed)
3 large eggs
1 cup of sweetened condensed milk
¾ teaspoon ground cinnamon
¾ teaspoon Tamika Scott's "Sweetener" Southern Fuse
1 cup of brown sugar (packed)
¼ cup of white granulated sugar
½ teaspoon salt
¼ teaspoon ground nutmeg
¼ teaspoon ground clover 1 teaspoon of lemon
1 teaspoon vanilla extract
¼ cup all-purpose flour

Directions

1. 4 hours before making your Pizie, prepare pie crust by adding all ingredients (except butter and water) to your food processor and pulse for a few seconds, until well combined.
2. Add butter to the food processor and pulse a few seconds until the mixture turns into large crumbs.
3. Gradually add water, 1 tablespoon at a time. Pulse a few seconds until your mixture turns into a bowl of dough.
4. Remove dough from food processor. Flatten it out with your hands into a round circular shape. Wrap it in plastic wrap and place in refrigerator for 4 hours or overnight.
5. Prepare Pizie filling, preheat oven to 350°F. In a large mixing bowl, add all ingredients except eggs and evaporated milk. Beat on medium speed, scraping the sides of the bowl often.
6. Add eggs and milk, beat on low speed until well incorporated.
7. Take Pizie Crust out of the refrigerator. Lightly sprinkle flour onto pie crust rolling mat. Roll out dough with a rolling pin. Make sure your crust is more prominent than your pie dish.
8. Carefully place the dough into the pie pan, pressing firmly against the bottom and sides. Trim edges around the sides with a sharp knife to fit your dish. Crimp edges all the way around with your fingers.
9. Pour filling into crust. Cover the edges of the crust with a strip of aluminum foil to keep it from browning too quickly.
10. Bake 60 minutes or until the knife inserted in the center comes out clean.

Princess Armani loves making different treats. The easiest one we have so much fun making is her Gooey Chewy Rice Krispies Treats. I want to share a few simple notes with you before making these gooey treats. First, make sure the heat isn't on a high when melting your marshmallows. High heat will make it hard. Please keep it low for extra gooeyness. Once marshmallows melt, remove them from heat. Marshmallows can burn, which would cause them to become hard. Please look at the date on your marshmallows. Marshmallows do get old and old marshmallows do not completely melt. When placing treats inside of the pan to set, DO NOT press down hard! This will cause the treats to harden while cooling. Gently spread them in.

Ingredients

*¼ cup of butter
(salted sweet cream)
6 cups of mini
marshmallows (or eight
regular size
marshmallow)
1 teaspoon vanilla extract
6 cups of Rice Krispies
cereal*

Directions

1. In a large non-stick skillet, over low to medium heat, melt your butter. Add marshmallow and gently stir with a greased spatula. Remove from heat.
2. Add vanilla and stir. Add Rice Krispies and gently stir until well coated.
3. Add parchment paper in a 9x13 pan. Transfer Treats on top of parchment paper. Allow cooling completely. Serve and enjoy.

Mika's Sweet Georgia Bread

Ingredients

Georgia Bread
1 cup Strawberries
3 (12oz) cans biscuits
1 cup granulated sugar
2½ teaspoon
cinnamon
1 tablespoon Tamika
Scott's "Sweetener" Fuse
¾ cup butter
Cooking
spray
¾ cup brown sugar

Southern Sweet Glaze
2 cups confectioners'
sugar
1 teaspoon vanilla extract
¼ cup butter
(melted)
4 tablespoons heavy
whipping cream or milk

Directions

1. Add 1 cup of sugar, "Sweetener" Fuse, and cinnamon in a medium food storage zipper bag. Shake well to combine.
2. Preheat the oven to 350°F.
3. Open biscuits and cut biscuits into quarter sizes.
4. Add biscuits to food storage bag, shake and coat.
5. Coat Bundt pan or bread pan with cooking spray.
6. Place dough evenly in pan.
7. Place butter and brown sugar into a saucepan. On medium-high, allow butter to melt.
8. Pour mixture over dough. Bake 40 minutes. When done, take out of the oven and allow to cool for 10 minutes.
9. Prepare Sweet Glaze. In a medium-size bowl, add confectioner sugar. Add your melted butter, 4 tablespoons of whipping cream, and vanilla extract. Stir to blend.
10. Beat with an electric mixer until creamy, add more whipping cream or milk if necessary for your desired consistency.
11. Rinse and cut your strawberries in half, set them on a paper towel to dry. Place strawberries on top of Georgia Bread.
12. Drizzle glaze on top of Strawberries and Georgia bread. Serve and enjoy!

When you think about donuts, the first thing that comes to mind is police officers. Coincidently, I love donuts, and I always wanted to be a police officer growing up. My dad was a Fulton County Deputy Sheriff, and every night when he came home, he entertained us with an exciting story about his day. He loved to protect, serve, and bring order to the communities. My father was also a deacon at the church we went to.

People constantly criticized him and asked how he could be a Christian and a police officer. My father always responded, "Who would you rather get stopped by, a saved or unsaved cop?" My father started his police career in the early '70s when segregation was in full effect. He was the only African-American police officer in his department. At times he felt the presence of prejudice from other officers, but he did not allow that to stop him from walking in his destiny. My father was called to a traffic stop where two (Caucasian) officers had arrested a man for aggravated assault one late evening. When my father arrived on the scene, the officers had the assailantl s arms behind his back. They opened the back door of my father's police car and put the criminal in the back seat. They told him to take him to the station and that they would be there shortly. As my father was driving to the police station, he began to minister to the man. Telling him how much God loved him and that he could change, and that God would forgive him of any wrongdoing he has ever done in his whole life. The man begins to confess to my dad that he beat up his girlfriend because he caught her cheating.

My father continued to minister to him. Then he had one more confession. He told my dad that he didn't have any handcuffs on and that he had a gun. He was going to shoot my dad in the back of the head before he showed him compassion. My dadl s heart started beating fast as he looked in the rear- view mirror and saw the gun in the manl s hand. The man put it on the floor and raised his hands and started crying and repenting. My dad pulled over, got the gun from the floor, and cuffed the criminal. And took him to the police station.

The two officers were written up with no consequences. And sadly, nothing has changed much since then. That's why after graduating high school, I wanted to go to college for my criminal justice degree to become a police officer. However, I was blessed to get a singing contract. So, I had to choose between college and X-scape, you already know what I decided. But it didn't stop my love for donuts. We always joke about cops and how much they love their donuts. So, dad, this is for you and all the good cops out there. Thank you for your service!

Mika's Old Fashion Buttermilk Donuts

Ingredients

2 cups all-purpose flour
1 cup granulated sugar
2 teaspoon baking powder
2 large eggs
¾ cup buttermilk
½ teaspoon cinnamon
½ teaspoon nutmeg
1 teaspoon vanilla extract
½ teaspoon salt
1 teaspoon Tamika Scott's "Sweetener" Southern Fuse
2 tablespoons of canola or vegetable oil
Powdered sugar (for garnishing)
Cooking spray

Directions

1. Preheat oven to 400°F. Spray 2, 6-cavity doughnut pans with nonstick cooking spray.
2. In a small bowl, whisk together the buttermilk, eggs, vegetable oil, and vanilla extract.
3. Whisk together the flour, Sweetener Fuse, granulated sugar, baking powder, cinnamon, nutmeg, and salt in a medium bowl.
4. Add the wet ingredients to the dry mixture and gently stir together until well combined.
5. Pour batter half-full, into doughnut pans. Do not overfill.
6. Bake 9-10 minutes or until done.
7. Remove from oven. Allow cooling completely before sprinkling with powdered sugar.

Mika's Sweet Candied Pecans

Ingredients

4-5 cups of halved pecans (unsalted)

1 teaspoon of Tamika Scott's "Sweetener" Southern Fuse

1 teaspoon of ground cinnamon

1 cup of granulated sugar

1 teaspoon of sea salt

1 tablespoon of pure vanilla extract (pure, no invitation)

1 (large) egg white

Directions

1. Preheat oven to 300°F.
2. Grease a large baking pan (no foil or parchment paper). Bake directly on the well-greased pan.
3. In a medium bowl, combine Sweetener Fuse, sugar, cinnamon, and sea salt. Place aside.
4. In a small glass bowl, whisk your egg white and vanilla until it becomes frothy.
5. Add your pecan halves to the frothy wet mixture, a half cup at a time to coat the nuts evenly.
6. Pour sugary mixture onto the pecans and thoroughly coat each piece.
7. Spread the pecans onto the prepared baking pan in a single layer.
8. Bake for 15 minutes, then stir.
9. Bake another 15 minutes and stir.
10. Bake 10 more minutes and stir.
11. Bake 5 more minutes.
12. Remove the candied pecans from the oven. (Pecans will continue to harden once pecans are out of the oven) Allow to cool for 5 minutes and enjoy.

Check In!

You are doing a good job!
Show me your best dish.
Take a photo and tag me.

@TheRealTamikaScott
#CookingWithTamikaScott

About the Author

Tamika Scott remains an essential brand in American culture for over **25 years**! Her successful, **Multi-Platinum** music career has gained her numerous prestigious awards with her R&B Group, **X-scape**. With over **20 million records sold globally,** Tamika has put in the work with XCSAPE, and established numerous chart-topping Billboard number 1 songs! **After reuniting with X-scape and touring 42 cities of sold-out arenas, Tamika** released her EP, **Family Affair,** with five original songs and one R&B classic, **"Go Outside in The Rain"**, with over one million streams.

This multi-talented, wife, mother, glam-Mother, and friend is adding **Author** to her many titles with the release of her cookbook, **"Cooking with Tamika Scott"**, published by **Hunter Publishing Group.** Between performing with her World-Renown group **X-scape,** her **Philanthropy,** cooking for family and friends, Tamika still found time to launch another business, **Tamika Scott's Southern Fuse seasonings,** in **Atlanta, GA. Tamika Scott's Southern Fuse** has **TEN** different spice flavors to awaken your taste buds. Like a melody to a song, each Fuse is sure to make music in your mouth, while adding depth and flavor to every bite! Whether you a vegetarian or meat lover, there is a fuse you can use!

Index

Index

Index